D0649003

CHILDREN OF DIVORCE

HELPING OTHERS IN
• CRISIS •
CHILDREN OF DIVORCE

JIM AND BARBARA DYCUS

David C. Cook Publishing Co.
Elgin, Illinois—Weston, Ontario

David C. Cook Publishing Co.
Elgin, Illinois—Weston, Ontario
Children of Divorce
© 1987 David C. Cook Publishing Co.

Scripture quotations, unless otherwise noted, are from the *Holy Bible: New International Version.* © 1978 by the New York International Bible Society. Used by permission of Zondervan Bible Publishers. Other quotations are from *The Living Bible* (TLB), © 1971 by Tyndale House Publishers, Wheaton, Illinois, also used by permission; and from the *King James Version* (KJV).

Excerpts from the following books are also among those used by permission:

Surviving the Breakup: How Children and Parents Cope with Divorce by Judith S. Wallerstein and Joan Berlin Kelly. © 1980 by Judith S. Wallerstein and Joan Berlin Kelly. Reprinted by permission of Basic Books, Inc., publishers.

Being a Single Parent by Andre Bustanoby. © 1985 by the Zondervan Corporation. Used by permission.

Caught in the Middle: Children of Divorce by Velma Thorne Carter and Lynn J. Leavenworth, © 1985. Used by permission of Judson Press, publishers.

Divorce and Separation: Context, Causes, and Consequences edited by George Levinger and Oliver C. Moles. © 1979 by The Society for the Psychological Study of Social Issues. Reprinted by permission of Basic Books, publishers.

The photographs contained on the cover and throughout this book are staged dramatizations and are for illustrative purposes only. These photographs do not depict actual persons engaged in the situations described in this book, nor are they intended to do so.

Published by David C. Cook Publishing Co.
850 N. Grove Ave., Elgin, IL 60120
Cable address: DCCOOK
Designed by Christopher Patchel
Photo by Bakstad Photographics
Illustrated by Jane Sterrett
Printed in the United States of America
Library of Congress Catalog Card Number: 86-070185

ISBN: 0-89191-345-9

We appreciate you: Marlene LeFever, Harold Ivan Smith, Deborah Cole, Alex Clattenburg, and others, who have encouraged and guided us into ministry among single parents and their children.

We love you: single parents and your children, who have let us share your burdens, experience your growth, and watch God's plan for your lives unfold.

CONTENTS

PREFACE

INISTERING TO CHILDREN WHOSE PARENTS ARE DIVORCED is like driving in a strange city without a road map. Our churches' traditional children's programs give us little guidance in handling these children's needs, and the rocketing divorce rate only makes matters worse. Yet many churches are realizing their failure to confront this issue. That's probably why you are reading this book. You are becoming aware of the need to help the *child* of divorce understand the *crisis* of divorce.

We want this book to become your road map to helping the children of divorce in your church and community. You will also discover ways to help single parents who are struggling to raise those children amid the confusion of their detoured lives. These parents and children alike need your help to reach their destination—becoming what Christ wants them to be.

Toward that end, this book will help you understand both the children of divorce and their parents. You'll find out how to start a ministry which will guide these single-parent families toward healing—and which will fit the philosophy and resources of your own church.

How much is such a ministry needed in your church? The following story may bring the answer home.

A little girl was busily showing a visitor her doll collection. The visitor asked, "And which of these dolls is your very favorite?"

The little girl replied, "I haven't shown you my favorite. I was afraid you wouldn't like her."

When the visitor assured her that he would, the little girl ran to get her favorite. She returned with a dirty, ragged, broken, worn-out doll. "This is my favorite dolly," she said.

"And why is she your favorite?" asked the visitor. "Why do you love her so much?"

The little girl replied, "I love her so much because if I didn't, nobody would!"

Can we do any less with the children of divorce? Their lives may seem broken and ragged. But we need to accept them as Christ would—unconditionally. Only then can we truly minister to them. If we do not reach out to them in love, who will?

Jim and Barbara Dycus

INTRODUCTION

WHY DO WE, THE AUTHORS, FEEL SO STRONGLY ABOUT the children of divorce? In part, it's because the tragedy of divorce has touched both our lives—in very different ways. The following accounts explain how.

Barbara's Story

These two words altered my life for all time: "I'm leaving."

I heard my father say those words one day as he walked down the stairs of our home with two suitcases in his hands. Those words signaled the end of a marriage that had begun almost 25 years earlier.

With those words, I became a child of divorce.

My father's parents had divorced when he was young, too. After he and my mother married, my father served as Sunday school superintendent; my mother was active in the women's activities at church. They took me to church for the first time when I was eight days old, and I was in nearly every service from then on. My parents were very proud of their church heritage and lived as nearly like Christ as they were able to live.

Then in 1959 our cozy Christian existence changed forever. My mother experienced an emotional upheaval for which she would accept no help, and from which she could not fully recover. She focused her frustration on her stable, 25-year marriage, and several confused months later that relationship was shattered beyond repair.

My parents were devastated by this development. They felt that a failure to live according to God's laws had removed them from His favor. They were unable to prepare my sister or me in any way for the changes the divorce would bring.

The night my father left, I did not know whether he meant he was leaving for a night, for a trip out of town, or forever. In the weeks and months to come I would be isolated by my hurt, having no one to reach out to me with healing. I felt as though I had been trapped in a nightmare.

The small, conservative church we attended was unable to accept this breach of conduct from two of its stalwarts. We were asked to leave the congregation. We left it and never returned.

That experience became the catalyst for my desire to help both the children of divorce and their parents to find healing for their hurts.

After graduating from Bible college in 1964, I served full-time for eight years as a commissioned Salvation Army officer. My ministry appointments included Divisional Youth Counselor for Wisconsin and Upper Michigan, Territorial Girl Guard Director for the central states, and Assistant Territorial Youth Secretary for the same region. Jim and I were married in 1973, and as a pastor's wife I have served as Sunday school superintendent and children's church coordinator. Since Jim and I began helping the divorced and single-parent family I have supervised our ministry to children.

Jim's Story

When I came to the Lord through the ministry of Teen Challenge in 1972, God's forgiveness wiped away my former life of heroin addiction, alcoholism, crime—and divorce.

Raised in an upper-middle-class family on the prosperous north side of Chicago, I was a budding baseball player and golfer by my early teens. But in 1955, at age 16, I took a turn down a dark path. A friend introduced me to marijuana; a year later I found myself addicted to heroin. It was a habit that would hold me in bondage for the next 13 years, even driving me to commit armed robbery to pay for the drug.

In 1960 my father was committed to a mental institution. A year later my mother committed suicide by jumping in front of a train. Overcome with guilt, feeling my rebellion had caused my mother's death, I spent the next year going to her grave at night with a folding chair and sitting there begging her forgiveness.

During the next 10 years I spent many months in hospitals, drug rehabilitation programs, and jails. But none of these changed me. I married, but the relationship fell apart a year later when I deserted my wife and one-month-old son. I would not see that son again for 22 years.

In 1970 my father died in the mental hospital; my drug-induced fog kept me from attending his funeral. In 1971 I was shot while robbing a Chicago drugstore, only to return to the streets after my release from jail.

By now I was in my 30s. Bone tired, empty, alone, longing for a family of my own, I was more than ready for a change. I entered a methadone program for addicts, and a social worker referred me to Teen Challenge. That marked my first encounter with Christ and my last bout with heroin. On January 21, 1972, in the chapel of Teen Challenge, I accepted Jesus and have been free ever since.

In 1973 Barbara and I married. Eventually we would have three children—Jimmy, Jackie, and Dinah.

From the moment I committed my life to the Lord, God gave me a desire to serve Him. I felt called to the ministry, but didn't see how God could get a man with my past into such a position.

Then, in the church that had welcomed me from Teen Challenge, I began a Sunday school class for single adults. It was the beginning of the ministry Barbara and I would have to singles. I accepted additional responsibility at that church until the senior pastor announced, "Jim, I need an associate pastor. God has shown me that you are my man." In 1979 I entered full-time ministry, serving as associate pastor of Belmont Evangelical Church in Chicago.

While at the church, Barbara and I began to see more and more divorced people coming through. Some would stay for a while, but most would move on. As a divorced person myself, I began to ask, "What are we doing to meet their needs right where they are?"

I had heard plenty of teaching on how God hates divorce. But I had never heard anything that would help divorced people "after the fact." It was then that God led us to start a ministry to divorcing and divorced people and their children.

We asked God how to design such a ministry. He directed us to John 8, the story of the woman taken in adultery, and John 4, the account of the woman at the well. In both cases, we saw that Jesus' approach was one of compassion and concern. He accepted the women just as they were; His greatest concern was for their present condition, not past mistakes.

We knew that divorced people suffer such pain partly because they have a hard time finding a place to heal and recover under an umbrella of love. We also knew the best place for them to rebuild should be the church. A pastor, board, and congregation who genuinely generate compassion could lead to the harvest of many hurting people.

God seemed to ask us, "What do you want?"

My reply was, "Give me the divorced as my inheritance!" Feeling strongly that divorced people need divorced heroes, I asked God to make me such a servant so that many would come to know wholeness in Christ. It was then that we founded Support Ministries, which focuses on helping divorcing and divorced adults and their children.

In 1984 I became pastor to single adults at Calvary Assembly in Winter Park, Florida, a church of over 6,000 with hundreds of single adults. Our work with Support Ministries continues in the form of specially designed workshops for single-parent families, and we travel extensively to conduct conferences and seminars for single adults and single adult leaders. We want to reach out to parents and children who are broken by the hurts of divorce and bring them to total recovery.

The Issue: Healing

The apostle Paul instructs, "You ought to forgive and comfort him [a brother gone astray], so that he will not be overwhelmed by excessive sorrow. I urge you, therefore, to reaffirm your love for him" (II Cor. 2:7, 8).

The issue here is not whether people should or should not divorce. God's standards for marriage never change. But the fact is that people *are* divorced. Our concern in this book is to describe how to minister to these broken lives.

The church must serve divorced and separated individuals. Those who form the caring, compassionate relationships needed for such service will soon discover that divorced and separated people are in pain. They are not looking for someone to "kiss it and make it better," but for someone to accept them as they are, understand what they are going through, and lead them to a place where the atmosphere of healing allows recovery.

This healing is exemplified in the recovery God promised the Israelite nation:

For I know the plans I have for you . . . plans to prosper you and not to harm you, plans to give you hope and a future. Then you will call upon me and come and pray to me, and I will listen to you. You will seek me and find me when you seek me with all your heart. I will be found by you . . . and will bring you back from captivity. I will gather you from all the nations and places where I have banished you . . . and will bring you back to the place from which I carried you into exile (Jer. 29:11-14).

Divorce has held so many people captive to their hurts. God is calling us, His church, to bring them back from their captivity so that He may reveal to them His plans for their lives. By His grace, He can use us to help heal the children of divorce.

CHAPTER ONE

VICTIMS OF
AN EPIDEMIC

D IVORCE HAS BECOME ONE OF OUR SOCIETY'S GREATEST threats to children. In 1985, for example, the divorce rate had reached such an epidemic level that 25 percent of all children in the United States were living in one-parent homes. The rest of the U.S. statistics are equally devastating:
- Half of first marriages end in divorce.
- Nearly two-thirds of second marriages end in divorce.
- There are 1.25 million divorces and 1 million desertions per year, approximately 3,562 divorces per day, 148 divorces per minute.
- Approximately 70 percent of couples divorcing have children under the age of 18.
- Of those who have divorced, 5½ million women and 3¼ million men have not remarried.
- About 65 percent of divorced fathers do not provide financial support to their families.
- There are 1,300 new stepfamilies every day, or 474,500 annually.

Has the meaning of these statistics settled into the hearts of churches? We think not. All too often the Church has failed to respond to the divorce epidemic. One 1980 study of California single-parent families (*Surviving the Breakup* by Judith S. Wallerstein and Joan Berlin Kelly, Basic Books) found that only 5 percent of the children were counseled or sustained by a church congregation or minister. Wallerstein and Kelly concluded:

Divorcing parents and their children have for some time been a population that is expanding explosively; yet its special needs are insufficiently recognized, little studied, and poorly served. . . .

Our findings pointedly highlight the children's unmet needs. . . . This ongoing need by the child for competent, nurturant parenting places a continuing demand on the parent who assumes full or major responsibility for the child's upbringing. In order to fulfill the

19

responsibility of childrearing and provide even minimally for the needs of the adult, many divorced families are in urgent need of a formal and informal network of services not now available to them in the community.

Mary L. Gendler, a psychologist who works with children of divorce, sees the problem more clearly than many churches do:

Although everyone involved in divorce is affected and seems to suffer to a greater or lesser extent, perhaps the most poignant victims are the . . . children . . . who are caught in their parents' decision to separate. These youngsters are deeply affected by a decision which they have not made and which they are powerless to stop. They must learn to cope, sometimes at a very young age, with major changes in relationships, life-styles, and often physical location. It must be remembered, also, that divorce is never a discrete event, but signals a sequence of changes that will continue throughout the history of the family *(The Wild World of Divorce, Puppet Plays with Children of Divorce and Separation,* an unpublished dissertation).

Those changes can also be transmitted from generation to generation. The hurt is compounded in the life of each family member. Researchers are beginning to document the fact that divorce runs in families. This tendency is woefully evident in Barbara's case, for example. In three generations of her family, 18 of 20 people were divorced once. Two were divorced twice. Only one, Barbara, has never been divorced and is currently in a first marriage.

The church must do what it can to break this tragic chain. The multiplied millions of children who have been directly affected by divorce will be among the parents of tomorrow. Unless their hurts are healed, their chances of becoming caring, effective, nurturing parents are greatly diminished.

Let the Healing Begin

Christians have not yet begun to scratch the surface of ministry to the 13½ million children in America alone who have been directly affected by divorce. God can heal the hurts of divorce, but His Church must become His hand of healing.

God's Word tells us to "Carry each other's burdens" (Gal. 6:2). This does not refer only to adult-size burdens; God recognizes the hurts of children, too. We believe Christ set the precedent for helping the suffering children of divorce when He said, "Let the children come to me, for the Kingdom of God belongs to such as they. Don't send them away!'' (Mk. 10:14, TLB)

We mentioned earlier that the divorce of Barbara's parents was a devastating event for the small country church they attended. For many years after the divorce became known, Barbara's Sunday school teachers did not communicate in any way with Barbara or her sister. More than 25 years passed before Barbara had the opportunity—at her mother's funeral—to speak with one of those teachers. With tears running down her face, the teacher told Barbara, ''I didn't know what to do!''

We have come to understand that teacher's dilemma. We recognize her frustration at not knowing how to help Barbara and her sister without seeming to condone the sin of divorce. But Barbara needed the church at that point in her life—and it wasn't there.

We cannot continue to let 13½ million children be trapped by their hurts. Nor can we neglect their parents by failing to let them know of God's healing power—and His promise of a future beyond divorce.

How to Begin?

How do we get beyond our paralyzing fears and doubts about divorce in order to reach children where they hurt most?

1. *We need to know God's Word.* In addition to understanding Biblical principles about marriage and divorce, we should know Scripture well enough to answer the questions the children of divorce often ask.

Barbara learned this lesson firsthand when she became a child of divorce. She had always looked to her church for answers, having never learned to search out and apply principles from God's Word. When her parents divorced, she felt as though the spiritual rug had been pulled out from under her feet. Desperate for answers, but no longer having access to her church leaders, she was left only with questions like, ''Why didn't God answer my prayers and put my family back together?'' ''Have my parents committed the unpardonable sin, and are they headed for eternal destruction?'' ''How real is Christianity if it fails me in my hour of deepest need?''

Barbara was fortunate; her faith in God's love and care turned her to Him and His Word, instead of away from Him. She clung to His promise in Jeremiah 29:11: ''For I know the plans I have

21

for you . . . plans to prosper you and not to harm you, plans to give you hope and a future.''

But many who face divorce have no foundation of faith on which to rebuild their lives. They desperately need someone to point to the Great Physician and to assist Him in applying the balm of His healing to their hurts.

2. *We need to understand the effects divorce has on children.* These insights from Arnold L. Stolberg and James M. Anker focus on the needs of elementary children:

> The psychological impact of divorce is well documented. Problems common to children of divorce already identified as having some special psychological needs are: higher rates of delinquency, enuresis [bedwetting], depression, aggressiveness to parents, sexual acting out and school problems. Significantly poorer cognitive performance and social interaction skills were found with children from single parent families. The perceptual experience of some children of divorce is one of self-blame, of feelings of being different from their peers, and of a heightened sensitivity to interpersonal incompatibility ("Cognitive and Behavioral Changes in Children Resulting from Parental Divorce and Consequent Environmental Changes,'' *Journal of Divorce,* Winter 1983).

On the problems of adolescent children of divorce, the same article had this to say:

> For adolescents, parental divorce has also been shown to have potentially serious adaptive consequences. As in younger children, increased impulse control problems and antisocial, aggressive behaviors have been reported for adolescents who experience family disruption due to divorce.

3. *We need to recognize the implications of divorce for our local churches and communities.* Divorce is not just a problem "out there." If 66 percent of the children in the United States are affected by divorce, then many of the kids in your Sunday school classes are among them.

This fact was brought home to us when Barbara, as Sunday school superintendent, was confronted by teachers who faced "discipline problems" in their classes. Barbara discovered that all the "problem children" lived in one-parent homes and had recently experienced the divorce of their parents.

One such child was three-year-old Amy, who would never sit still and listen in class. One day Barbara visited the home where

Amy and her three sisters and mother lived. Barbara had brought the makings of a Thanksgiving dinner, which we were giving to each of the single-parent families in our church. As Amy's mother opened the refrigerator door to put away the food, Barbara noticed that the only other food in the refrigerator was a jar of mustard! Amy's mother apologized for the fact that she often had to send Amy to Sunday school without breakfast.

These "discipline problems" were children who needed someone to reach out to them and offer healing for their hurts. And they were in *our* church.

When we conducted a poll of our congregation, we were amazed to discover that 34 percent of the children in our church were children of divorce. Suddenly we saw that one-third of our kids were in pain because of an experience for which we had not prepared them—and from which we were not helping them recover.

4. *We need to define the role we believe God wants us to take in helping children of divorce and their families.* This will take great soul-searching. Can we hate the sin of divorce, yet love the divorced family? Can we work through the mistaken conviction that ministry to the divorced means condoning divorce and weakening the Church's stand on marriage and the family? What are we going to do with the divorced after they are healed? Can we believe they are loved by God as is every other believer? Can we help them reach their full potentials in Christ?

What about the children? If a Sunday morning relationship is all you feel God is asking you to have with children of divorce, then you may not be ready for ministry to them. These little ones have already suffered feelings of rejection and loss, and will need more unconditional acceptance and love than you can transmit during a Sunday school lesson. They need to know you will not leave them nor limit your commitment to them.

Joey, for example, was reported to us as a real problem. He was constantly disruptive, would not respond to correction, and paid no attention to the Sunday school lesson. His disruptions were part of the reason why Joey's teacher was giving up the class. Soon a male college student took over. He began to take the class on outings, went out for pizza with them, and often took one or two of the boys in the class home to spend Sunday afternoon with him. He recognized the special need Joey had for a male role model; as he began to minister to Joey, the boy's heart opened up. He responded to the teacher's care as a sponge responds to water.

Soon Joey was whispering to others in the class who were disruptive, "You don't have to act like that!" He blossomed under the ministry of that caring, giving young man. When the church presented a Christmas musical that year under the college student's direction, Joey played the lead!

A Sunday morning relationship was not enough for Joey. Neither will it be enough for the children of divorce in your church and community.

Needed: A Tender and Skillful Hand

Jesus set the example for ministry to hurting children. Consider His actions and words:

> Jesus called a small child over to him and set the little fellow down among them, and said ". . . any of you who welcomes a little child like this . . . is welcoming me and caring for me. But if any of you causes one of these little ones who trusts in me to lose his faith, it would be better for you to have a rock tied to your neck and be thrown into the sea" (Matthew 18:2-6, TLB).

How can we welcome the children of divorce rather than alienating them from Christ and His Church? We need to treat them with sensitivity and skill.

Consider the historical example of how Lord Delaware led the colony of Virginia to maturity. Through the efforts of Sir Walter Raleigh, Virginia had been settled in 1585. The little colony had suffered many disappointments. It had been deserted in 1586 and recolonized in 1587, only to see all its residents perish in a famine soon after. In 1607 Jamestown was settled, but still faced violent animosities among its leadership, a war with native Indians, famine, disease, and anarchy. In 1609 the settlement was again abandoned. Then Lord Delaware arrived to reestablish the colony. This is what happened:

> But it was not the will of Heaven that all the labour of the English in planting this colony, as well as all their hopes of benefit from its future prosperity, should be forever lost.
>
> A society so feeble and disordered in its frame required a tender and skillful hand to cherish it, and restore its vigour. This it found in Lord Delaware: he searched into the causes of their misfortunes, as far as he could discover them amidst the violence of their mutual accusations; *but instead of exerting his power in punishing crimes that were past, he*

employed his prudence in healing their dissensions, and guarding against a repetition of the same fatal errors [italics ours].

Under such an administration, the colony began once more to assume a promising appearance (from *The History of the Discovery and the Settlement of America* by William Robertson, Harper Brothers, 1835, as quoted in *The Christian History of the Constitution of the United States of America: Christian Self-Government* by Verna M. Hall, Foundation for American Christian Education, 1960).

Lord Delaware's example typifies our vision of ministry to children of divorce and their parents. Just as he reached out with healing to the hurts, rather than simply punishing past offenses, so must we.

Only through Christ can the children of divorce find real recovery. That's why the Church can no longer close its eyes and hope "the problem" will go away.

What an opportunity we all have to share the news that God can heal the hurts divorce has caused! How thrilling it can be to see the victims of the divorce epidemic begin to thrive and move into their full potentials in Christ. What an opportunity, what a challenge—and what a responsibility!

CHAPTER TWO

CASE STUDIES

E ACH CHILD OF DIVORCE IS UNIQUE. WE CANNOT LUMP THESE
children together and treat them in the same way. And
because they will not all respond identically to our love,
we need to offer that love over and over again—until it can
tunnel through the hurt to touch the heart.

This chapter will illustrate the uniqueness of these children, as
well as point out several characteristics they often exhibit. The
following real-life case studies (names and circumstances have
been altered to maintain confidentiality) are representative of six
types of children who are among those encountered by the
Christian who ministers to families of divorce.

Andy: The Angry Child

Every child of divorce has been angry. Most probably have
difficulty with that emotion. After all, divorce has thwarted the
child's desire for both parents to stay together, and as a result he
or she feels angry.

How can the angry child be recognized? Spotting overt
expressions like temper tantrums or screams is easy, but
suppressed anger, described by psychologists as "passive-
aggressive behavior," is harder to spot. Yet it can be more
damaging over time than open, explosive behavior.

Nine-year-old Andy had begun attending our single-family
workshops with his mother, Jan, who had been divorced for 18
months. Neither Andy nor Jan had seen Andy's father since he
had left; the latter did not contribute financially to the support of
the family. The marriage had been a very destructive experience,
and Jan had not recovered. Nor had Andy, whose unstable
homelife and parents' divorce had caused him a great deal of
emotional stress.

Andy and his mom had suffered several years of physical and
emotional abuse by Andy's father, a volatile, angry man,
especially when he was drinking heavily. The abuse had left its

mark on Andy, but he had internalized his confused emotions. He struggled with feelings of love and hate for his father, as well as guilt over his father's abuse of his mother; somehow Andy felt responsible.

Andy hid these feelings from his mother. He compensated for his mother's hurt by appearing to be docile, obedient, and calm at home.

At school, however, Andy's behavior had been very different. Since the start of the school year he had been through two or three teachers. Each reported that Andy was disruptive, belligerent, vindictive, and abusive. They would no longer allow him to remain in their classrooms and had advised his mother to seek professional help for him.

Andy acted up at the workshops, too. He went to any extreme to disturb what was going on, often verbally attacking other children and refusing to participate. But he continued to attend. Gradually he improved his behavior when asked to, though he still tried to manipulate those around him.

Apparently enjoying the activities and acceptance he found in the class, Andy began to participate willingly when he was granted the special status of "teacher helper." But when asked to discuss how he felt about his parents' divorce, he would again be disruptive or would turn off to the class.

Then came the night when the class roleplayed. Andy was to play the part of a boy whose father deserted the family and never returned. After acting out the story, he was to add his opinion of what should happen to that father.

Andy calmly acted out the story. But when the time came to insert his "verdict," he suddenly tensed and blurted out in a rage, "That man ought to die for what he did to his family!"

For the first time Andy's buried anger toward the father who had deserted him surfaced. Barbara held Andy close, letting the boy's anger pour out.

Even though Andy didn't turn into a well-disciplined, manageable student right away as a result of releasing his anger, he continued to open up during the next several weeks. He let his mother and Barbara talk with him about his pain. He became a willing participant in his own healing process, accepting his hurts and dealing with them.

How can we help children like Andy? First, we need to understand the nature of anger. People become angry when (1) they feel threatened; (2) they have learned to get their way by being angry; (3) they are frustrated; or (4) they have been hurt. Some children will express anger passively, indirectly, with whining, crabbiness, withdrawal, a critical spirit, resistance to parental rules or discipline, or self-isolation. Other children may use more open, direct expressions. Without help, the latter may even turn to antisocial or criminal activities.

Counselor and author Archibald Hart makes this comment about anger in children:

Allowing anger to be openly and frequently expressed is also not the healthiest way to resolve it. This pattern, if repeated often, can breed an "angry personality"—someone who is consistently mad at everything and who believes that the rest of the world has been conveniently provided as a punching bag for his or her feelings.

No one who is angry has a right to take his anger out on someone else. The New Testament is very clear in its teaching on this point. Paul tells us, "If it be possible, as much as lieth in you, live peaceably with all men. Dearly beloved, avenge not yourselves . . ." (Rom. 12:18, 19, KJV). Parents have a responsibility to teach their children how to cope effectively with their anger and how not to let it become a destructive force in their lives (From *Children and Divorce* by Archibald D. Hart, Ph.D., © 1982; used by permission of Word Books, publisher, Waco, Texas).

Each child must learn to express built-up anger and then control it whenever it resurfaces. This process can be illustrated by the steam radiators some older homes still have; once in a while it is necessary to release a portion of that steam by "bleeding" the radiator. Comfort in the home is maintained by controlling the flow of steam and directing it in a positive channel.

After Andy was confronted with his unresolved anger, he recognized it, released it, and searched for more positive responses. Our role as Christian leaders in this healing process is to help children like Andy understand their negative feelings and learn more positive responses. Because Andy was able to do this, he recovered.

Peter: The Abused Child
Sometimes the turmoil of divorce erupts into physical violence, as it did in Mary Jane's family.

"If someone doesn't stop me, I'll beat him until I don't have any strength left!'' Mary Jane exclaimed to several people who had seen her arguing with her 10-year-old son, Peter. Peter had run off, leaving her standing alone, shaking violently, crying.

Her comment was especially significant because she said it at church, following a single-adult activity. She was not really promising violence to her son; she was for the first time making a public plea for help with her own battered emotions.

An abused child herself, Mary Jane had run away from home in her teens and gotten married—to a man who also abused her and their two sons. He was unfaithful, and often disappeared for days at a time. Finally, after seven years, he had divorced Mary Jane and remarried immediately.

Slowly Mary Jane had begun to put her life back together. She found work, supported her boys, and began to attend our church. Eventually she gave her life to Jesus Christ. But she and her boys had not dealt with any of the emotions they had accumulated while they had been abused.

Soon after they started to attend church, Peter and his brother acted up in their Sunday school classes. Their teachers reported the behavior to Mary Jane, who confronted the boys. They in turn were defiant, which angered Mary Jane, and she began to physically abuse them.

Mary Jane couldn't understand why she or her boys were behaving as they were. The fact was that for the first time, the three of them were in a caring, loving environment. The emotional walls they had erected to hide their hurts were starting to crumble, and the intense, negative feelings from the past were pouring out.

Mary Jane felt so guilty about abusing her boys that she hid her behavior for months. But that night at church it all came out. As she stood there shaking and sobbing, she was pleading for help.

Since that night, Mary Jane and her sons have begun to deal with their pent-up emotions. They are not completely healed, but are firmly on the road to recovery.

How have the members of this single-parent family learned to overcome their emotional hurts? They became involved in a network of caring Christians who were willing to show support on a regular basis. Mary Jane received counseling from Jim. Peter and his brother joined our children's workshops, where they learned to understand and deal with their feelings. They developed trusting, caring relationships with their instructors, and responded to the support of other single-parent children.

Melissa: The Child of Separation

Melissa had just completed a drawing of her family. Her teacher was using the activity to determine how the children in her class felt about their families. As Melissa turned in her paper, she started crying. When the teacher bent down and asked what was wrong, the little girl sobbed, "I don't know where my mommy belongs in the picture!"

Melissa is not a child of divorce. She is a child of separation. Her mother deserted Melissa's father four years ago, leaving him with three children to raise alone. A devoted Christian, Melissa's father believes God will restore his family. He has decided to stand in faith and wait for his wife to return—even though she has not contacted her family since she moved out.

To the casual observer, the father seems to be coping well with his decision. Melissa's older brother and sister also appear to believe that God will miraculously return their mother to them. But what about Melissa? Can her seven-year-old understanding and emotions cope with waiting for a miracle?

To recover from divorce, a child needs a rapid return to stability and the chance to adapt to the changes divorce has brought. But for the child in a long-term separation situation, these two processes cannot take place.

Because Melissa's father is waiting for the marriage to be restored, their life-style is temporary—for an indefinite period. His goal of stability will be reached only when his wife returns. Adjustment to the present situation is not his goal, nor does he want his family to adapt to the changes separation brought. This means Melissa *cannot* put the experience behind her.

It's no wonder Melissa couldn't decide her mother's place in that family drawing. She may feel caught in an emotional tug-of-war between hope and reality—or disloyal to her mother, unable to believe the woman will return. She may even feel guilty, thinking her mother's failure to return is due to a lack of faith on her own part.

What can we do for children like Melissa? At times our role will be to assure her that God can bring her mother back. But sometimes we may need to help the family let go of false hope and face reality regarding the missing parent.

31

Melissa has not yet been allowed to go through this process. Recently she sat beside me in a church service. As I placed my arm lightly around her shoulder, she whispered, "You feel like a mommy."

I whispered back, "Do you miss your mommy, Melissa?"

Immediately the girl stiffened, moved away, and whispered, "She'll be back!"

Matthew: The Rejected Child

Matthew was an energetic five-year-old when he began attending our support meetings with his mother. His parents had divorced before Matthew was born. His father, now remarried, visited Matthew and his older brother irregularly and contributed financially to the family's support.

Matthew's mother had never released herself emotionally from her ex-husband. In fact, Matthew had been conceived *after* the divorce, when his father was continuing a physical relationship with Matthew's mother as well as with his new wife.

Even at five years of age, Matthew knew he didn't have the same kind of father/son relationship many of his friends in two-parent families had. When he became good friends with our son Jimmy, who was his age, Matthew envied the relationship between Jim and Jimmy. After a counseling session between Jim and Matthew's mother, Matthew came into the office, ran over to Jim's desk, climbed up on his lap, and said, "Will you be my daddy?"

Later Matthew and Jimmy were playing in the basement of the church when Jim walked through. Immediately Jimmy ran to Daddy, who lifted him up and swung him around in a display of father/son affection. As Jim lowered Jimmy to the floor, he heard a commotion and glanced at Matthew. He was amazed to see that Matthew had run over to his mother and thrown himself on the floor in an outburst of temper.

"Lois, what happened?" Jim asked.

"Don't you know?" she replied. "Matthew saw Jimmy run to you, and he doesn't have a daddy. Seeing Jimmy with his daddy disturbed him so much that he wasn't able to control his emotions and threw a fit."

Still another incident graphically revealed Matthew's longing for a "regular" father/son relationship. When his older brother was hospitalized, Matthew stayed in our home for a few days.

During this time he grabbed every opportunity to bask in the attention Jim gave him. The first evening as we tucked the boys in bed, Jim kissed Jimmy and said, "Good night, son."

Jimmy replied, "Good night, Daddy."

Then Jim kissed Matthew and said, "Good night, Matthew."

Matthew grabbed Jim in a bear hug and said, "Good night, Pastor Daddy!"

For the next several days Matthew had the benefits of a "regular" daddy.

At the end of Matthew's visit, Jim presented all the kids with a small gift; Matthew's was a package of sweat socks. "These socks are from my pastor daddy," Matthew told his brother later. For several weeks after this, each time Matthew saw Jim, he would run up and whisper, "Remember when you were my daddy?"

Children of divorce—especially young ones—desperately need consistent, caring role models. Matthew found such a model in Jim, and thrived as a result. But that kind of relationship generally cannot be created during a Sunday school hour, nor will it develop during a quick "Hello, how are you?" after class. It takes time, given repeatedly, until the child learns to trust the adult.

Scott: The Deserted Child

Jim picked up the phone. A man on the other end of the line asked, "Are you Jim Dycus?"

"Yes, I am," Jim replied.

"I'm Scott Dycus, your son!" the voice said.

Suddenly events of the last two decades flashed through Jim's mind. Scott *was* Jim's son, the son Jim had not seen for 22 years—since the boy had been one month old. That was when Jim had deserted his son and wife.

As noted in the introduction to this book, Jim had been a heroin addict when he deserted his wife and child, leading to divorce. Then God had miraculously intervened in Jim's life, delivering him from his dependency on alcohol and drugs. Jim married, had three children, and entered full-time ministry. But he did not know the whereabouts of his first family.

Then came the day when his *son* found *him*. Jim had believed God would restore a relationship with his son. But thinking about how he would react had not prepared him for the actual experience of talking with Scott—and seeing him.

"Daddy," Scott said on the phone that day, "I don't want anything from you, except that all my life my dream has been to meet my father."

One month after that phone call, Jim waited at the train station to meet his son. He wondered how Scott would respond to a father who had deserted him. But his fears were dispelled when Scott walked off the train and into Jim's arms with the words, "Daddy, I love you."

Jim wondered how love could exist, seemingly with no foundation. Where was the expected hostility and bitterness caused by rejection? As the days went by and there was no evidence of any of these negative feelings from his son, Jim finally brought up the subject.

"Scott, why don't you hate me?" he asked. "How can you possibly love me after all I did to you when I deserted you?"

Scott replied, "Daddy, all my life it's been my dream to get to know my father. My mother and my grandmother have always positively reinforced my love for you. They told me that even though you had many problems, underneath it all you were a good man and would have shown your love to me if you could. They told me how much like you I was and that you would be very proud to have me for a son."

Jim and Scott were fortunate. Unlike some single parents, Scott's mother had kept alive the seed which would someday blossom into a meaningful, loving, father-son relationship. She encouraged Scott to love his father. How important that is to a relationship broken by desertion and divorce!

Parents and children caught in such broken relationships need to recall the example of Abraham, "Who against hope believed in hope . . . He staggered not at the promise of God through unbelief; but was strong in faith, giving glory to God" (Rom. 4:18, 20, KJV).

Traci: The Wounded Child

Twelve-year-old Traci stood at our Single-Family Graduation Banquet and sang the song she had written during the weekly sessions:

Sometimes things happen we can't foresee,
And they just seem too big for me.
Then my heart feels cracked in two,

But God always knows what to do.
It's a crack in half that's been
put back together again,
Put back with God.

As Traci sang, her mother had tears running down her face. We could recall how she had remarked when classes began, "I don't think Traci really needs these classes. I was divorced 11 years ago when she was 18 months old, and she wasn't affected by our divorce."

Traci *had* been greatly affected, however. She had never faced her hurts, which had remained bottled up inside her.

Traci's father had remarried immediately after the divorce and moved to another state. While there wasn't any overt hostility or bitterness between Traci and her dad, there was no solid relationship either. In the ten years immediately following the divorce, Traci and her two older sisters had seen their father only four or five times.

Things had been hard for Traci's mother after the divorce. She had no job, but was forced to assume responsibility for financial obligations her ex-husband had left behind. Shortly after the divorce she had also had two emergency surgeries, each requiring months of convalescence.

Not coping well with the emotional devastation of divorce, Traci's mother had begun to frequent bars. "I wasn't an alcoholic, or an extremely heavy drinker," she would recall later, "but the atmosphere of the bar scene became as addictive to me as the alcohol could have been. I tried to escape from myself in this way." She also became involved with drugs and was sexually promiscuous.

She thought she had hidden her life-style from her three girls. But she realized otherwise when her oldest daughter became involved with drugs and promiscuity, quit school, and at age 17 moved into an apartment with a boyfriend.

In 1983 Traci's mom overdosed on drugs, going through a nightmarish drug trip in which she saw the destructive path of her life. She returned to church with her girls; she and Traci and her middle daughter gave their lives to Christ. He began to mend their hurts, and soon they were involved in our single-family workshops.

Traci's mother remembers that during the first four or five weeks of classes, the family went through a time of "tearing

35

down emotions and breaking down walls. For some reason I had always felt that from the day of the divorce the person that would be the least affected in this family was my youngest daughter, Traci. I thought that because she was only 18 months old and had never really had the chance to know her father since he was never home, that she would not be old enough to miss him or to care about the breakup.''

But Traci was wounded. During the sixth week or so of classes, the girl came into her mother's room and said, ''Mother, I want to read you my song that I wrote.''

Her mother read the words, then asked, ''What's the 'crack in half'?''

Traci replied, ''Mommy, it was my heart!''

For the first time her mother realized how deeply Traci had been hurt. ''I cried in gratefulness that God had seen our need, and He had been able to do something about it even when I couldn't,'' she recalls.

A healing process began for the whole family. Animosity between sisters ceased. Rivalry gave way to love for one another. As the kids began to heal, Traci's mom did, too.

One evidence of this healing came at Christmas. When the holiday rolled around, Traci's family still had no money, but determined to have a ''recycled'' Christmas. Family members mended each other's clothing and repaired furniture and other household goods, then took these to the older sister's apartment. At last Traci's family was working together.

Before long the older sister left her boyfriend and returned home. Eventually she received Christ as Savior.

The last verse of Traci's song holds part of the key to healing the wounded children of divorce:

Just look around and what do you see?
It's God's great big family.
What's minus one when you can have
A ton of family?

It's a crack in half that's been
put back together again,
Put back with God.

Andy, Peter, Melissa, Matthew, Scott, and Traci represent many of the children of divorce you are likely to meet as you minister. Each child carries a unique set of needs—and requires a unique response. But all wait for churches like yours and ours to act as Christ's hand of healing. To paraphrase another song:

Jesus loves the little children
Who have faced their parents' divorce.
Hurt, rejected, lonely, tough—
Jesus' love is quite enough.
Jesus loves the little children of divorce!

CHAPTER THREE

THE SEASON OF DIVORCE

G OD'S WORD TELLS US, "YOU HAVE BEEN BOUGHT AND paid for by Christ, so you belong to him" (I Cor. 7:23, TLB). Christ called us "more valuable to him [God] than many sparrows" (Mt. 10:31, TLB).

God has placed a high value on people, and that includes the children—and parents—of divorce. They may be scarred and broken, but to God they are priceless. That's why it's so important to prepare to help the single-parent family cope with its crisis. In this chapter we want to point out Biblical and psychological principles that will aid you in doing that.

Principles alone, of course, will not build the bridges divorced families need to reach the futures God has for them. The principles must be applied. As Velma Thorne Carter and Lynn J. Leavenworth observe in their book, *Caught in the Middle: Children of Divorce* (Judson Press):

In thinking about the thousands of families we have counseled, we could estimate that three-quarters of them have been reasonably active in some religious community prior to the separation or divorce, but of this number, few of them appear to have experience in relating the articles of their faith to the major decisions and shaping experiences of their lives in any conscious way. To affirm that God sustains life, that God's love is a paradigm for love may be affirmed in creedal statements in religious settings without those insights becoming significant factors in the flow of life itself. It is when the press of negative circumstances is upon us and we have to take the religious dynamics into the marketplace of human experience that we realize how "academic" or how "ecclesiastical" our religious faith has been in the past.

In the personal discovery of basic religious faith, the beleaguered parent finds the foundation for building hope and love, and in the process he or she develops a framework for coping.

We can see, then, that helping divorced families means guiding them to discover God's answers for themselves.

Putting the Pieces Together

One of our treasured possessions is a crazy quilt Barbara's great-grandmother made. It is truly a work of art, made from swatches of wool and velvet, beautifully embroidered with designs and flowers. The quilt's history has been passed down from generation to generation—for each swatch tells a story.

One piece of fabric, for example, came from Barbara's great-grandfather's wedding suit. Another was part of her great-grandmother's wedding dress. Still another was salvaged from the burial dress her great-grandmother made for a two-year-old daughter who died of smallpox.

That quilt is much more than a thing of beauty. Begun with "leftovers," it has become a record of a family's daily struggles and joys. It is a work of art created from the pieces of life's experiences, many of them symbolizing detoured dreams and broken hopes. The great-grandmother who made that quilt knew that even negative experiences can combine to create something beautiful. She wrote in her diary on January 1, 1879:

If we cannot use the sickle,
We can gather in the sheaves;
We can gather with the gleaners
What the skillful reaper leaves.

On May 8, 1879, she wrote:

Lord, what my talents are I cannot tell,
Still Thou shalt give me grace to use them well,
That grace impart, the blessings will then be mine,
But all the power and all the glory Thine.

The lives of single parents and of children of divorce are like that crazy quilt. Each piece—each life experience—alone may seem a meaningless fragment, without design. Yet as the pieces are put together in the framework of God's grace and power, a work of art emerges. Wholeness replaces brokenness, worth replaces worthlessness, and beauty replaces devastation.

"But though God has planted eternity in the hearts of men, even so, man cannot see the whole scope of God's work from beginning to end" (Eccl. 3:11, TLB). We cannot see the ultimate design of our lives. But that does not mean the design is not there. To help children of divorce and their parents build a framework for coping, we must help them see the Designer at work in their lives.

40

The Season of Divorce

There is a time for everything, and a season for every activity under heaven: a time to be born and a time to die, a time to plant and a time to uproot, a time to kill and a time to heal, a time to tear down and a time to build, a time to weep and a time to laugh, a time to mourn and a time to dance, a time to scatter stones and a time to gather them, a time to embrace and a time to refrain, a time to search and a time to give up, a time to keep and a time to throw away, a time to tear and a time to mend, a time to be silent and a time to speak, a time to love and a time to hate, a time for war and a time for peace (Eccl. 3:1-8).

In a sense, these verses summarize the single-parent experience. They remind us that life is full of changes, good and bad, and that we are continually passing through these changes. Right or wrong, many families will pass through the "season" of divorce; we must help them understand the changes it brings, and find the joy that follows sorrow.

In the third volume of his *A Commentary on the Whole Bible,* Matthew Henry sees the hand of God in all kinds of changes:

Those things which to us seem most casual and contingent are, in the counsel and foreknowledge of God, punctually determined, and the very hour of them is fixed, and can neither be anticipated nor adjourned a moment.

Some of these changes are purely the act of God, others depend more upon the will of man, but all are determined by the divine counsel. Everything under heaven is thus changeable, but in heaven there is an unchangeable counsel concerning these things (p. 995, Fleming Revell Publishers).

Knowing that God understands and makes sense of the changes brought by divorce can be the foundation for learning to cope with these changes. Though Ecclesiastes 3:1-8 does not speak specifically to the problem of divorce, some of the "times" listed there make a useful outline of the principles parents and children of divorce—and those who work with them—need to understand.

A Time to Be Born

Children are a heritage from the Lord, a reward from Him (Ps. 127:3). Both parents and children need to remember this, especially during the turmoil of divorce and its aftermath.

God loves to give gifts to His people—valuable gifts. His gifts are never intended to bring ultimate harm or sorrow; they are meant to enrich our lives, to make us better than we would have been otherwise. Children are such a gift.

Many divorced parents struggle with the demands of raising their children. Many feel inadequate and wonder whether their children might be better off with someone else. Some Christian single parents, feeling overwhelmed, have considered turning their children over to non-Christian ex-spouses. These Christian parents need to recognize their children as good gifts from a loving God.

God has a purpose for each child's life. He has given that child to a specific family as a first step in bringing that child to his or her full potential.

Likewise, the child of divorce needs to see the value God places on him or her. Psalm 139:15, 16: "My frame was not hidden from you when I was made in the secret place. When I was woven together in the depths of the earth, your eyes saw my unformed body. All the days ordained for me were written in your book before one of them came to be."

God wants the parent and child of divorce to understand that His gift of that child was good *before* the season of divorce, is good *during* that season, and will *remain* good long after the season has passed.

In *Caught in the Middle: Children of Divorce* (Judson Press), Velma Thorne Carter and Lynn J. Leavenworth quote a single mother who discovered this truth:

> I remember that day out there on the river bank when we discovered Psalm 139. It really registered with me that God not only knows everything about me—even before I was born—but also everything about my children before they were born. I felt the strongest sense of relief when that meaning came to me. I don't have to go on hiding, nor cringing, nor pretending. I can be myself; God knows me and is with me. The load simply slipped off my shoulders.

A Time to Plant

Christian parents—even divorced ones—have a Biblical responsibility to educate, cultivate, and nurture their children until those children reach maturity. J. Richard Fugate, in *What the Bible Says About Child Training* (Aletheia Publications), points out the following:

> Children need an authority figure. If parents do not provide the

needed leadership, their children will seek it elsewhere. Without firm leadership in the home, children will find someone outside the family who will tell them what to do. Children desperately need someone whom they can follow and to whom they can give their allegiance. . . . They will find a replacement if the parents abdicate their position.

It should be no surprise that leaderless children respond to cults, such as the Moonies and the Jones groups, street gangs, or revolutionary movements. These counterculture groups all have one thing in common—they demand followership. They each provide strong leadership, teach and enforce rules, and set a purpose for the life of the follower. Dare we as parents offer less?

Parental responsibility includes, but goes far beyond, physical care—as the following Bible passages make clear:

If anyone does not provide for his relatives, and especially for his immediate family, he has denied the faith and is worse than an unbeliever (I Tim. 5:8).

These commandments that I give you today are to be upon your hearts. Impress them on your children. Talk about them when you sit at home and when you walk along the road, when you lie down and when you get up. Tie them as symbols on your hands and bind them on your foreheads. Write them on the doorframes of your houses and on your gates (Deut. 6:6-9).

I will utter things, things hidden from of old—what we have heard and known, what our fathers have told us. We will not hide them from their children; we will tell the next generation the praiseworthy deeds of the Lord, his power, and the wonders he has done. He decreed statutes for Jacob and established the law in Israel, which he commanded our forefathers to teach their children, so the next generation would know them, even the children yet to be born, and they in turn would tell their children (Ps. 78:2-6).

A Time to Uproot

Divorce brings an uprooting, an instability that causes children distress. This uprooting can be far more traumatic than some have been willing to admit. As Judith S. Wallerstein and Joan Berlin Kelly report in *Surviving the Breakup* (Basic Books):

We have learned that a child's early response to divorce and separation is not governed by any balanced understanding of the issues that led to the parents' decision. Nor are the children much affected, if at all, by living in a community with a high incidence of divorce. Instead, at the time of the parental separation the child's attention is riveted entirely on the disruption of his or her own family, and he is intensely worried about what is going to happen to him. Whatever its shortcomings, the family is perceived by the child at this time as having provided the support and protection he needs. The divorce signifies the collapse of that structure, and he feels alone and very frightened.

God created marriage and the family, instituting the family as the best garden for growing godly children. Divorce disrupts that principle. That's why divorce is so devastating to children; God's design for their nurture has been disrupted.

Recovery from this spiritual uprooting will not come until the child is under the protection of a parent who is following God's principles for that family. Single parents must deal with this issue, committing themselves through God's grace to the Biblical principle of training their children according to God's plan.

"Has not the Lord made them [husband and wife] one? In flesh and spirit they are his. And why one? Because he was seeking godly offspring" (Mal. 2:15).

A Time to Kill

Giving up the dream of "resuscitating" his parents' failed marriage can help the child move more quickly into recovery. Nearly every child of divorce struggles with a desire to reconcile the family long after all real hope of doing so has disappeared.

Wallerstein and Kelly describe this struggle:

The poignant fantasies of reconciliation that preoccupied youngsters at every age can be understood as ways to restoring the family in order to help stave off the acute pain of loss. The hope, the wish, and sometimes the expectation that parents would reunite is at its height at the time of separation, and was a vivid fantasy for over half of the children. In their games, no single child in the entire group played separate homes or even separate bedrooms for the divorcing parents. Children happily restored the family in the playhouse by placing father and mother in one bed, together, with their arms tightly woven one around the other. Older children tried, sometimes indirectly, to bring about or even force the reconciliation they desired.

Where hope is well founded and reconciliation is possible, we need to dedicate our efforts to counseling with the parents in order to restore the marriage. But when that is not an option, we must help the child let go of the desire for something the parents have determined can never be. The child who will not let go of this fantasy is held captive to the destructive season of divorce.

A Time to Heal

Children of divorce hurt! They have wounds which need healing. They and their parents need our help to find that healing.

One of the greatest healing therapies God ever gave human beings is forgiveness. Without it we would live defeated lives, held in bondage by our guilt and failure. The parents and children of divorce need to know that they can be forgiven and forgive others; they don't have to feel as if they belong in the bargain basement of life.

The story of the adulterous woman brought to Jesus, recorded in John 8, provides an example of God's forgiveness. Instead of penalizing the woman, Jesus forgave her sin. He encouraged her to rise above that failure and begin living a new kind of life.

We can help the victims of divorce to rise above their failures and sins by pointing out the nature of God's forgiveness:

1. *Forgiveness is a gift from God.* Why did God invent forgiveness? Because people chose their own way in place of His perfect way. "Yes, all have sinned; all fall short of God's glorious ideal" (Rom. 3:23, TLB). We have *all* offended God by our failure to measure up to His ideal. For us He invented forgiveness—the road by which we move back into His favor.

2. *Forgiveness is complete.* "For I will forgive their wickedness and will remember their sins no more" (Jer. 31:34). "As far as the east is from the west, so far has he removed our transgressions from us" (Ps. 103:12). God created the two-step process of forgiving and forgetting. He considers the restoration to favor complete when He has taken the two steps.

God wants us to take those steps as well. He gives us the option of practicing spiritual forgetfulness. He wants us to move beyond our failures after He has forgiven them, and put the failures of others behind us as well.

3. *Forgiveness is a memorial service and a birth announcement.* "If any man be in Christ, he is a new creature: old things are passed away; behold, all things are become new" (II Cor. 5:17, KJV).

To us the words "passed away" indicate that a funeral has taken place. All a new creature can do about his or her failures after forgiveness is to hold a memorial service! We don't have

45

any squatter's rights to go on living in sin if Christ has forgiven us.

If "all things are become new," that creature isn't even the same person anymore! That person can send out his or her own birth announcements. God has completed the work of forgiveness by birthing that person anew—as fresh and innocent as a newborn baby.

Jim, for example, began a new life when God forgave all his sins. The heroin addict/alcoholic/thief he used to be has disappeared. We thank God that we don't have to get up in the morning to find hypodermic needles in the sink, or empty whiskey bottles under it. We don't walk into our living room and see stolen goods. Jim is a new creature in Christ.

Knowledge of forgiveness and new life in Christ is also crucial to parents and children of divorce. Their recovery hinges on it.

A Time to Tear Down

The King James Version calls this "a time to break down." Now *there's* a term people in crisis understand. Divorce can stress parent and child to the breaking point.

How can we ease this stress? The following two-step strategy should help:

1. *Encourage parent and child to believe in the hopeful, new future God promises.*

Therefore, since we have been justified through faith, we have peace with God through our Lord Jesus Christ, through whom we have gained access by faith into this grace in which we now stand. And we rejoice in the hope of the glory of God. Not only so, but we also rejoice in our sufferings, because we know that suffering produces perseverance; perseverance, character; and character, hope. And hope does not disappoint us, because God has poured out his love into our hearts by the Holy Spirit, whom he has given us (Rom. 5:1-5).

In these five verses alone, God has offered the faithful believer a future of justification, peace, access into grace, hope of the glory of God, rejoicing in suffering, perseverance, character, hope, love, and the presence of the Holy Spirit. The vision of such a positive future can reduce the stress of despair for children and adults involved in divorce.

2. *Teach divorced families positive responses to negative circumstances.* The apostle Paul was in a most undesirable circumstance—jail—when he wrote the following:

46

Do not be anxious about anything, but in everything, by prayer and petition, with thanksgiving, present your requests to God. And the peace of God, which transcends all understanding, will guard your hearts and your minds in Christ Jesus. Finally, brothers, whatever is true, whatever is noble, whatever is right, whatever is pure, whatever is lovely, whatever is admirable—if anything is excellent or praise-worthy—think about such things. I can do everything through him who gives me strength (Phil. 4:6-8, 13).

Living these verses can turn defeated divorce victims into positive people. Members of divorced families can begin to "think about such things" by meditating on selected Scriptures. To help them achieve the following changes in attitude, urge them to study the passages listed after each change:
a) From grief to hope (Ps. 31:14-23; Jer. 30:17)
b) From turmoil to stability (Gen. 21:17-20; Mk. 4:35-41)
c) From unnecessary guilt to assurance of mercy (Ezek. 18:20; I Jn. 1:9)
d) From rejection to acceptance (Mt. 18:2, 5, 10; Ps. 139:16)
e) From anger to peace (Phil. 4:4-9)
f) From depression to confidence (Rom. 8:18-39)
g) From inferiority to worth (Jn. 3:16-18; Eph. 2:4-7)
h) From inflexibility to willingness to adapt and change (Phil. 3:10-14; Rom. 5:1-5)
i) From denial to dealing with reality (Isa. 43:18, 19;)
j) From fear to security (Josh. 1:8, 9; Jer. 29:11-14)
k) From loneliness to companionship (Ps. 68:6; Mt. 28:20; Heb.13:5)
l) From confusion to understanding (Isa. 48:17)

A Time to Build
The church must be the construction company for the child of divorce. "Unless the Lord builds the house, its builders labor in vain" (Ps. 127:1).

Many mental health professionals have also concluded that the church has the best opportunity for meeting the needs of these children.

So why aren't we doing it? We may say, as did the Sunday school teacher who didn't speak to Barbara for 25 years after Barbara's parents were divorced, "I didn't know what to do." But it is our business to find out how to build up children and parents who have suffered through divorce.

Ezekiel 34:2-6 (TLB) might as well have been addressed to
church leaders and congregations who have failed to reach out to
these hurting people:

Son of dust, prophesy against the shepherds, the leaders of Israel,
and say to them: The Lord God says to you: Woe to the shepherds who
feed themselves instead of their flocks. Shouldn't shepherds feed the
sheep? You eat the best food and wear the finest clothes, but you let
your flocks starve. You haven't taken care of the weak nor tended the
sick nor bound up the broken bones nor gone looking for those who
have wandered away and are lost. Instead you have ruled them with
force and cruelty. So they were scattered, without a shepherd. They
have become a prey to every animal that comes along. My sheep
wandered through the mountains and hills and over the face of the
earth, and there was no one to search for them or care about them.

All too often we are ready to ignore or even tear down the
person who has suffered the effects of divorce. It is time to start
building.

A Time to Laugh . . . a Time to Dance

It probably goes without saying that the season of divorce
involves "a time to weep . . . a time to mourn." This is normal,
and should not be denied as "unspiritual." But knowing that
God forgives the guilty and creates new life can and should usher
in a time of great joy for the victims of divorce.

Our church has built a great sanctuary to seat 5,000 people.
During the construction process huge steel beams weighing 180
tons each were raised by gigantic cranes to rest atop concrete
pillars. When the time came for those cranes to release the
beams, there was great rejoicing; the pillars took the weight.
Similarly, divorced and separated parents can rejoice in the fact
that their children can take the weight of life and build successful
futures in Christ—despite the end of a marriage.

Furthermore, divorce doesn't have to take the joy from a
child's life indefinitely, causing him to hang his head in sorrow
and hurt. By sharing and modeling God's grace we can help that
child lift his or her head high and build a life beyond the divorce
experience.

A Time to Embrace

Children of divorce need the church's embrace—an embrace
of unconditional acceptance and love.

The Book of Philemon provides the example of Onesimus, the runaway slave accepted by Paul. The apostle's urging of Philemon to welcome Onesimus reminds us why this acceptance is so important:

1. *Acceptance releases one to become useful.* "Onesimus (whose name means 'Useful') hasn't been of much use to you in the past, but now he is going to be of real use to both of us" (v. 11, TLB).

2. *Acceptance frees one from bondage.* "No longer only a slave, but something much better—a beloved brother" (v. 16, TLB).

3. *Acceptance allows us to become one, as we are one in Christ.* "Give him the same welcome you would give to me if I were the one who was coming" (v. 17, TLB).

4. *Acceptance glorifies God.* "Give me joy with this loving act and my weary heart will praise the Lord" (v. 20, TLB).

5. *Acceptance paves the way for further recovery.* "I've written you this letter because I am positive that you will do what I ask and even more!" (v. 21, TLB)

This attitude of acceptance was displayed by Marty, a man in our church. One Wednesday evening, after the church programs had been dismissed, two boys were talking in the foyer about a father/son camp-out planned for the weekend. The first boy said, "Doesn't the camp-out sound like a blast? I can't wait!"

The second boy, whose parents had been divorced, replied with great enthusiasm, "Yeah! It sure does!"

"Ha, ha, ha," taunted the first boy. "I get to go with my dad. You won't be able to go because you don't *have* a dad!"

Instead of being devastated, the second boy quickly responded, "Oh, yes, I am—Marty's taking me!"

Marty, one of our children's workshop leaders, was a warm, loving, compassionate person who carried a big burden for kids of divorce. He had not said he was taking this little boy on the camp-out yet. But the boy knew how much Marty loved him. Marty had developed such a trusting, caring relationship with him that he was sure Marty would take him. Sure enough, Marty did.

The church needs fewer people who would stigmatize the children of divorce—and more, like Marty, who will accept them.

A Time to Search, a Time to Give Up

Divorce brings confusion and change to parents and children.

49

It requires searching for and adapting to a new life-style. It means giving up some things which have been part of life for a long time.

We need to help victims of divorce in their search, helping them to understand the changes and to restructure their lives as God gives them direction. Biblical principles like these should be shared with them and expanded upon:

"I am the Lord your God, who teaches you what is best for you, who directs you in the way you should go" (Isa. 48:17).

"Trust in the Lord with all your heart and lean not on your own understanding; in all your ways acknowledge him, and he will make your paths straight" (Prov. 3:5, 6).

A Time to Keep, a Time to Throw Away

The child of divorce has to adapt to a new relationship with both his parents. He has a right to keep their love and support, and to throw away the frustration, hostility, and anger created by the failing marriage.

Toward that end, the church must help parents and children of divorce to develop sound relationships. God's Word provides several principles for us to impart:

1. *The home needs an atmosphere of respect.* "Honor your father and mother. . . . Fathers, do not exasperate your children" (Eph. 6:2-4).

2. *Good parental relationships are rewarding.* "The father of a righteous man has great joy; he who has a wise son delights in him. May your father and mother be glad; may she who gave you birth rejoice!" (Prov. 23:24, 25).

3. *There are penalties for poor family relationships.* "A child left to himself disgraces his mother" (Prov. 29:15).

4. *Following good parental guidance leads to a child's prosperity.* "My son, do not forget my teaching, but keep my commands in your heart, for they will prolong your life many years and bring you prosperity" (Prov. 3:1, 2).

A Time to Tear, a Time to Mend

Matthew Henry, in his *A Commentary on the Whole Bible,* elaborates on these phrases in this way: "A time to rend the garments, as upon occasion of some great grief, and a time to sew them again, in token that the grief is over."

It may seem elementary, but the intense grieving period

divorce brings does not have to last forever. The church must offer hope by affirming repeatedly to the victims of divorce that *divorce is a season*. It has a beginning, but it also has an end. With God's help the single parent and the child of divorce can put the pieces of their lives back together.

A Time to Be Silent, a Time to Speak

Sometimes talking about one's divorce experience is unnecessary, even detrimental. But sometimes telling one's story, especially to another hurting person, can speed healing to that person's hurts.

Barbara learned this firsthand. Many times she would have loved to speak her mind about what happened to her and her family. But nothing positive would have resulted. When she stood before her mother's casket and faced the members of the church her family had been asked to leave when her parents divorced, she wanted to let them know her feelings. She was angry that after 25 years of silence, those people would appear when it was too late to make a difference in her mother's life. She was indignant that her former spiritual leaders had failed to give her hope when she needed it. She wanted to say, "It's too late now. Why are you here?"

But to do so would have caused more brokenness. By keeping silent she was able to open the door to reconciliation.

On the other hand, for Barbara to avoid speaking to churches today about their need to reach out to children of divorce would be an even greater failure. Her experience tells her that those children need the church. If speaking out can bring reconciliation, it will be for the glory of God.

A Time to Hate, a Time for War

Single parents and children of divorce, if they care about God's way, will ultimately reach a time of hating, or warring against, divorce. They will hate the devastation of divorce. They will recognize it as a stronghold of the devil. Ideally, they will also begin to tear that stronghold down.

" 'I hate divorce,' says the Lord God of Israel" (Mal. 2:16). Why does God hate divorce? Because of what it does to the lives of people He loves, as well as what it does to His institution of marriage.

That is why we hate divorce, and why we intend to make war

on it. God's people, responding to God's message, can do something about the rising destruction of divorce. In addition to opposing it, we can reach out to those who have experienced it and help them to recover. They, in turn, can join the battle.

God hates divorce. But it is vital to remember that God *loves* the *child* of divorce. He also loves the adult who has been through divorce. So must we.

A Time for Peace

How can the child of divorce make peace with his or her experience? By growing through it, and by leaving the season of divorce behind to enter the season of recovery. Thanks to the forgiveness and love of God, peace is a possibility for the child of divorce, for the single parent. And we can be part of it.

CHAPTER FOUR

QUESTIONS AND ANSWERS

HELPING CHILDREN OF DIVORCE OFTEN MEANS FACING SOME tough questions from their parents. How will you answer the distraught single mother or father who comes to you with concerns about a hurting child?

This chapter contains some questions frequently asked by parents whose children are suffering the effects of a divorce or separation. The answers we offer are by no means the only ones you could give, but they summarize what we would want those parents to know.

1. *My husband recently deserted us, and I don't know how to tell my children about it. What should I do?*

It's hard to confront the whole issue of divorce and separation with our children. Yet it's vital for us to do so in a way that will cause them the least emotional upheaval.

Children, even very young ones, sense many of the changes divorce and separation bring. Here are some important things to remember when we talk to them about these changes:

a) *We must be honest with children about a divorce.* Trying to shield a child from the facts will ultimately hurt him or her. Facing reality will speed recovery.

b) *We must prepare ourselves to answer our children's questions.* It takes patience to answer as often as some children ask. But we must do so, and with as many facts as we can give them.

c) *We must give children an opportunity to express their feelings.* Too many times we are tempted to say, "You're a big boy (or girl). Don't cry anymore about this." We need to create an environment that encourages open communication.

d) *We must keep reassuring our children that we love them.* The words we use to tell our children about the changes are important, but the way we say them is even more important. Children especially need both verbal and physical affection at this time, and they need to know that regardless of their emotional responses they will be unconditionally accepted, loved, and cared for.

e) *We must learn to trust God with our children.* Ultimately He is their Healer.

2. *My son feels guilty about my divorce, and thinks he is somehow responsible for it. Why?*

These feelings are a very common response for children of divorce.

Most children, after all, feel hostile toward their parents at times, and find themselves wishing those parents harm—even if only for a moment. Usually the harm never happens, but what if it does? When a divorce or separation occurs, those wishes of harm may seem to have "come home to roost." The child thinks he or she has caused the disaster and feels guilty.

Other false assumptions can cause trouble for children at this time. To a child, parents represent stability and strength; Mom and Dad can fix anything, take care of "owies," and keep away those big kids down the block. Mom and Dad are always right and strong. So when divorce happens and Mom and Dad can't handle it, the child may think, "This must be my fault, since I'm the only one who does wrong things."

One three-year-old girl, for example, caught her divorced mother crying one day. The girl ran off, only to return with a big rock. Thinking she had caused her mother's pain, the girl said, "Here's a rock you can 'frow' at me, Mommy!"

While guilt is a normal reaction, the child needs to recognize that *the divorce belongs to his or her parents.* The child had nothing to do with it; it is a grown-up problem.

3. *Why does my daughter act as though she doesn't care about the divorce?*

For some children, divorce is so traumatic that they protect themselves from the hurt by adopting a noncaring attitude.

Just as a computer reaches its memory capacity and shuts down, a child can reach his or her emotional capacity and shut down responses. While this is normal, the child will need help to find an outlet to express his or her feelings.

Debbie, 11, was one such child. Her parents had divorced when she was eight. As we interviewed her for a video presentation on children of divorce, we asked her, "How do you feel now about your parents' divorce?"

"Oh, I never have felt bad about it," she said. "Everything is fine. I don't think it ever bothered me very much."

Later in our taping, however, we asked her the same question—in different words. We said, "How do you think children feel when their parents divorce?"

This time she replied with great emotion: "Oh, I think they feel so bad they just wish they could *die!*"

The third-person, nonthreatening question had allowed her an outlet to finally express deep feelings of loss she had held in for years.

4. *My son refuses to stop believing that his father will return home to us, and that everything will be as it was before. How can I help him accept the reality that this can never be?*

For many children of divorce, the hope for a remarriage between Mom and Dad will continue long after all the actual possibilities of such have faded away.

The younger the child, the more he or she gains a sense of stability and security from the two-parent family relationship. If that relationship ends, he feels loss and instability, and his "security blanket" is removed.

Our oldest child used a security blanket when he was an infant. That blanket finally became little more than a collection of holes! But Jimmy clung to it as though his very life depended on it. Finally, in desperation, we bought a new blanket just like the old and tied the two together. We hoped he would transfer his affection for the old to the new, so that we could get rid of the eyesore. But he would have nothing to do with either blanket as long as they were tied together. Thus we were able to get rid of both blankets and move on.

The child of divorce needs *time* to get rid of his security blanket of false hope. A new relationship and a new life-style will take getting used to before the child's sense of belonging and security returns.

5. *My 10-year-old daughter insists that she hates her father and never wants to see him again. How can I help her?*

Expressing hatred for either parent is another common response to the crisis of divorce.

55

Negative feelings toward the absent parent arise from a child's deep sense of loss and rejection. The child feels deprived of a relationship with that parent, may suffer from loneliness, and probably feels unloved by that parent. To retaliate, the child strikes back by expressing hatred.

The wise parent will, without comment, allow the child to express these negative feelings. The "hated" parent should affirm to that child that leaving home has not changed his or her love for the child. Once those feelings have been expressed and the parent's love has been affirmed, the child's sense of loss can slowly diminish and the relationship can be restored.

A hurting child may also express hatred for the custodial parent. After all, this parent must now do all the disciplining and keep finances under control. This may mean depriving the child of some things he or she has been used to having, which the child will likely resent. In this case, too, allow the child to express the negative feelings; understand them as reactions to change. Continue to provide unconditional acceptance and an atmosphere of open communication, which will help the child to overcome these feelings.

6. *Why shouldn't I tell my son what a rotten father he has, and all the bad things his father did to me?*

Many times a parent with unresolved hostility toward an ex-spouse wants to get even by turning the child against the ex-spouse or by using the child to transmit hostility and contempt.

This can only hurt the child, causing compounded insecurities and confusion. The child may even think, "Because Daddy is so bad, I must be, too. I'm Daddy's son, and everyone says I'm just like him."

Children must not be forced to choose the love of only one parent. They need *both* parents. In some cases a good relationship with the absent parent may be more hope than reality, but we need to keep that hope alive. There are positive qualities about each parent that the other needs to affirm constantly to the child. Parents must avoid placing on a child's shoulders the burden of having to determine who was right and who was wrong in the failure of the marriage.

A trial judge once said, "If I had to name one unpardonable sin of a parent toward a child, it would be the act of one person trying to make a child hate the other."

There is another reason why a parent should not turn a child against an ex-spouse, and it should be of special concern to Christian parents. A child's concept of God is affected by his view of his parents. J. Richard Fugate writes as follows in *What the Bible Says About Child Training* (Aletheia Publications):

Parents are the symbol and representative of God's authority to their children. The way parents handle their rulership is the way children will begin to think about God and all other authorities under God. Parents are in a very crucial position in the child's life. Let us look at how a child thinks. If he sees his parents are fair, then he will consider that God must also be fair. If his parents punish for wrong, then God will punish for wrong. If his parents care for him, then God must care for him. If his parents respect and obey God's Word, then he must respect and obey God. If his parents mean what they say, then God must mean what He says.

How does a child learn to love God? Isn't it by loving his or her earthly father? The child who has no father, or whose father does not demonstrate godly qualities, needs help to develop the right view of God. This can be done by teaching the child about God from Scripture, and by providing other good, adult role models. But denigrating an ex-spouse in a child's eyes will not help the child develop a sound view of God.

7. *I'm worried that my son will not understand his role as a male now that he has no father around. What can I do?*
Children learn about the roles of mother and father, husband and wife, from observing their parents. A son, for example, develops his masculinity by watching and imitating his father's behavior. This process can be disrupted by removing a parent from the home.

Many single parents worry about this, fearing their children may somehow be hindered from reaching mature manhood or womanhood. To prevent this, the single parent and the church should work together to provide substitute role models for their children. Many qualified men and women in our churches have the time and desire to do this. It is up to the church to activate the troops!

This should be a high priority for those who want to minister to children of divorce. It isn't hard to give a little boy an appropriate hero to look up to as he grows and matures. Just as that boy will grow up emulating negative heroes if we allow it, he can be given the opportunity to imitate the positive behavior of a Christian man.

To begin this kind of role modeling, churches should explore Christian "big brother" and "big sister" programs, the involvement of Sunday school teachers whose classes include single-parent children, and the planning of activities that mix single-parent children with volunteer role models.

8. *My son wants to talk constantly about the divorce. This is so hard for me! I would rather just forget it and go on with my life. Must we rehash this over and over?*

Children often work out negative emotions and confusion over changes in their lives by talking about their feelings.

It's hard for you when you want to explain it once and move on with your life, but your child needs the opportunity to *feel*. Otherwise he may internalize his negative emotions, only to find them erupting at a later and less opportune time.

Barbara's parents, for example, were unable to talk over their divorce with her. She had no one to turn to, and remembers well the agony of those pent-up emotions and unanswered questions. She coped as well as she could for a number of years. But the day came when she went to her dad and said, "I've got to have some answers. You've got to level with me and help me understand what happened and why you and Mom divorced." She remembers the intensity of her emotions at the time, and the release she felt when she could finally talk about it with her father. Fortunately for her, the release of emotion had positive results.

Unfortunately for other children of divorce, the release is at times a negative one with disastrous results. Juvenile delinquency, school behavior problems, depression, and suicide can all result from repressed emotions which become too big for the child to handle.

Give your child time and opportunity to verbalize his feelings. Keep the door to communication open and encourage him to begin to talk about the positive aspects of his situation. Help him to see that while his life has changed, change does not have to be hurtful or disappointing.

9. *I can't help feeling that I've caused irreparable harm to my child by getting a divorce, even though the marriage was an*

*explosively negative situation. Will my child ever recover from
the damage?*

Many divorced parents are burdened by guilt, fearing divorce
is such a traumatic event that their children will forever be
damaged by it.

For the child of divorce whose parents have just ended an
extremely negative marriage, however, divorce and its
subsequent changes may actually afford a chance to recover and
mature. Dr. J. Louise Despert, in her book *Children of Divorce*
(Doubleday), writes, "It is not divorce, but the emotional
situation in the home with or without divorce that is the
determining factor in a child's adjustment. A child is very
disturbed when the relationship between his parents is very
disturbed."

It is especially reassuring for Christians to remember God's
concern for their children's well-being. Psalm 139:16 says, "All
the days ordained for me were written in your book before one of
them came to be." God knew every moment and circumstance
of our lives before we were conceived. He knew every moment
of a single parent's life, and decided that parent was the best
person to raise that child—even though He knew in advance
every negative situation parent and child would face.

But what about the statistics that show divorce "runs in
families"? Is a child bound to repeat the sins and mistakes of his
or her parents? After all, Numbers 14:18 (KJV) says, "The Lord
is longsuffering, and of great mercy, forgiving iniquity and
transgression, and by no means clearing the guilty, visiting the
iniquity of the fathers upon the children unto the third and fourth
generation."

This verse tells us that while God is long-suffering, merciful,
and forgiving, He will not clear the guilty one who chooses to
remain guilty. Furthermore, that person's sin will affect his or
her offspring for up to four generations. We need only look at
our world to know how often this is true; we see alcoholics who
have alcoholic children, child abusers begetting child abusers,
rebellious parents with rebellious sons and daughters.

Yet there is another link in our understanding of this truth. For
the guilty one who repents of his guilt, God's grace is sufficient
to break the pattern of sin and remove its penalty.
"Consequently, just as the result of one trespass was
condemnation for all men, so also the result of one act of

righteousness was justification that brings life for all men''
(Rom. 5:18).

God's grace restores the guilty to favor with God. It also
breaks the chain of sin in families. We do not anticipate that our
son Jimmy, for example, will become an alcoholic or drug
abuser or divorced person just because his father did. Jimmy will
be held accountable for his sins only.

Yet you ask, "Why does the son not share the guilt of his father?''
Since the son has done what is just and right and has been careful to
keep all my decrees, he will surely live. The soul who sins is the one
who will die. The son will not share the guilt of the father, nor will the
father share the guilt of the son. The righteousness of the righteous man
will be credited to him, and the wickedness of the wicked will be
charged against him. But if a wicked man turns away from all the sins
he has committed and keeps all my decrees and does what is just and
right, he will surely live; he will not die. None of the offenses he has
committed will be remembered against him. Because of the righteous
things he has done, he will live. Do I take any pleasure in the death of
the wicked? declares the Sovereign Lord. Rather, am I not pleased
when they turn from their ways and live? (Ezek. 18:19-23).

10. *I'm concerned about the way my daughter's self-esteem has
obviously lowered since her father and I divorced. How can I
help her feel better about herself?*

The trauma of divorce seems to be a fertile breeding ground
for low self-esteem. Most children of divorce are victims of this
problem. Parents and church leaders need to recognize this and
help restore a sense of value to these children.

Here are some steps which can help:
a) Give the child opportunities to succeed. The tasks you give
her should be ones she can accomplish, and which will give her
positive feelings about her success.
b) Help the child recognize her talents and abilities. Guide her
into areas which allow her freedom to express herself through
her special abilities. Help her to see the positive characteristics
she has, and to use these to greater advantage.
c) Recognize the child's accomplishments.
d) Maintain open communication and friendliness with the child.
Provide unconditional acceptance and love in your home.
e) Give the child opportunities to develop good relationships
with her peers. Help her learn to be a good friend. Give her
freedom to have times of fellowship and fun with her friends.

f) Continue to express love to the child, even if recovery takes time. Allow her sense of stability to return. Let her work through her negative feelings about divorce. Be flexible and understanding.

g) Encourage the child to see his or her worth as one of God's valued creations—apart from accomplishments and circumstances. As opportunities present themselves, share with the child Scriptures that make clear the worth of every person. Helpful passages include Genesis 1:26-31; John 3:16; and 1 John 4:10-11, 19.

CHAPTER FIVE

COUNSELING THE VICTIMS

F EW WOULD DENY THAT CHILDREN OF DIVORCE ARE LIKELY to feel stress, depression, and a lowered sense of self-esteem. But are the emotional effects of divorce and separation on children so intense that counseling is needed? Consider this observation from *Surviving the Breakup* by Judith S. Wallerstein and Joan Berlin Kelly (Basic Books):

> For children and adolescents, the separation and its aftermath was the most stressful period of their lives. The family rupture evoked an acute sense of shock, intense fears, and grieving which the children found overwhelming. Adding significantly to the widespread distress of the children is the fact that many of them face the tensions and sorrows of divorce with little help from their parents, or anyone else, for during the critical months following the separation parental care often diminishes, not because the parents are necessarily less loving or less concerned with their children during divorce, but because the radical alterations in their lives tend to focus their attention on their own troubles.

Who will rescue these children? Is it strictly a job for psychologists and social workers? No. Christian leaders who take the time to understand these children's needs can uniquely aid them through counseling.

It may come as a surprise to know that pastors can be especially helpful to those who are going through a divorce crisis:

> There is evidence that when people seek help with a marital problem they are more likely to consult a clergyman than a psychiatrist, psychologist, or marriage counselor. Moreover, there is some evidence to the effect that people who consult clergymen are likely to be more satisfied with the assistance that they receive than those who see a psychotherapist ("The Role of the Clergy in Divorce: An Exploratory Survey," Janet Weinglass, Kenneth Kressel, Morton Deutsch, *Journal of Divorce*, Vol. 2, No. 1, Fall 1978).

The same article, relying on a national survey done in 1960

63

(since more recent statistics were not available), helps us understand the opportunity pastors have to aid divorced families:

Of respondents who had sought help with a marital problem: 42 percent consulted a clergyman with 70 percent reporting they were helped; 11 percent saw a psychiatrist with 59 percent of them reporting being helped; and 8 percent saw a marriage counselor with 33 percent of them reporting being helped.

A survey completed by Dr. Arnold Stolberg of the University of Virginia's Department of Psychology named four groups of people divorced persons thought helpful during the divorce adjustment. Starting with the most helpful, they were:

1. The church
2. Family and friends
3. Medical professionals
4. Psychiatrists or psychologists

These studies indicate that when the church is willing to help the family of divorce to recover, it is often successful. Yet most of the time the church simply doesn't get involved. In their study, for example, Wallerstein and Kelly found that "fewer than 5 percent of the children were counseled or sustained by a church congregation or minister."

The church can't afford to miss this ministry opportunity. That's why, in this chapter, we will suggest outlines for counseling the single-parent family. We'll concentrate on (1) helping parents lead their children toward recovery, and (2) counseling the child directly.

In his *Christian Counseling: A Comprehensive Guide* (Word Books), Gary Collins writes, "Sermons and intellectual discussions about divorce often are informative, but rarely do they convey the pain that so often accompanies a broken marriage." In other words, we need to leave the pulpit to find the source of pain these people feel.

A friend of ours who lost a leg in the Korean War has often said, "My leg hurts today!" We thought that strange, considering the fact that he has no leg. But then we learned of "phantom pain"; the limb is gone, but the pain lingers on.

Children of divorce have also lost part of themselves, and the pain lingers on. Through counseling we can help them deal with the source of pain.

Serving the single-parent family through counseling is not

always easy, however. As we wrote in our self-published *Divorce Recovery Program Guide*:

Ministry to single-again individuals is time-consuming and energy-draining. Many single-again persons have such an overload of unmet needs that they are desperately seeking someone who can help them grow through the needs. This need for counseling must be a consideration *before* ministry is initiated. Otherwise, we will introduce needy people to the hope of recovery and healing—but fail to give them a treatment plan which will lead them to full recovery and wholeness.

In the same book, we listed five problems to be aware of when starting a counseling ministry to the victims of divorce:

1. You may experience a few false starts before all systems say "go." Keep going. Be sure to develop realistic and functional goals based on your people's specific needs.

2. Some will come to you for help which you are not equipped or trained to give. Some will make demands of you or the group which are inappropriate for the type of ministry you feel God wants you to have.

3. At times this ministry can become so demanding that you will feel other areas of your work are threatened. You will need to seek the wisdom of the Holy Spirit to help you prioritize your time.

4. Some of your church members will feel anxious over this type of ministry. Many aspects of this ministry are unsettling and confusing to the conservative church attender. You will need to educate your congregation to the needs of single-again people as you begin.

5. Some of your counselees will fail to progress as they should. Divorced and separated people are very vulnerable, and at times will make mistakes in their relationship building. You will need to be prepared to help deal with these mistakes in such a way that your total ministry is not threatened.

Some Counseling Goals

What is counseling the single-parent family all about? Gary Collins defines Christian divorce counseling this way:

At the risk of oversimplification we might conclude that Christian marriage counseling attempts to keep marriages together and help couples develop smoother, more fulfilling Christ-centered marital relationships. In contrast, Christian divorce counseling attempts to help an individual or couple separate from a marriage in a way that is consistent with Biblical teachings, and with a) a minimum of pain or destruction to themselves and to others, including the children, and b) a maximum of growth and new learning (from *Christian Counseling: A Comprehensive Guide* by Gary Collins, © 1980; used by permission of Word Books, publisher, Waco, Texas).

Wallerstein and Kelly, meanwhile, elaborate on the kinds of counseling divorced families need:

People need help as the marriage declines and at the point that they decide to divorce. They don't know how to tell their children and . . . often neglect to do so. They need help in providing proper support to the children during the transitional time. They need help for themselves and their children, in preparing for the many changes (economic, social and psychological) which are expected in the post-divorce family and in setting up appropriate joint plans for continued care of the children when at all possible.

Counseling the single-parent family is a challenge for the Christian leader. A number of churches are beginning to help single parents in this way, but the children of divorce need special attention, too.

For that reason the counseling outlines in this chapter mainly address the child's needs, not those of the parent. They attempt to help the single parent with parenting as well as aiding the child directly. The "awareness meeting" outlines in chapter 6 could prove helpful in a counseling program as well; some of its sessions could serve as a framework for individual counseling in addition to group meetings. Feel free to adapt these as needed to fix your counseling style and church program.

What are our goals in counseling the victims of divorce? With children, we want to do the following:

1. Avoid the development of negative behavior and coping patterns;

2. Help the child understand the grief process;

3. Help the child understand normal reactions to divorce, and to identify personal emotional responses to his or her parents' divorce; and

4. Help the child develop skills for adapting to his or her situation.

With parents, we want to do the following:

1. Work toward recovery from divorce and maintain effective parenting skills;

2. Help the parent understand the common problems and needs of children of divorce; and

3. Help the parent establish meaningful communication with the child about the child's needs.

Finally, our goal for the whole single-parent family is to correct family patterns that encourage problem-causing emotions or behavior.

Counseling the Single Parent: Six Sessions

Our first six counseling sessions are meant for use with the single parent. Each session should help the parent aid the child's recovery. If needed, you may want to provide or subsidize child care so that the single parent is free to attend.

SESSION 1: THE PARENT'S INITIAL INTERVIEW

During this first session, you'll want to cover as many of the following 10 steps as possible.

1. Clarify the goals of your counseling sessions.

2. Briefly describe the three basic stages of divorce. These are as follows:

a) The Emergency Room Stage, in which the shock begins to take effect;

b) The Surgery Room Stage, in which the divorced person begins to adapt to changes brought about by the crisis of divorce; and

c) The Recovery Room Stage, in which the person moves into healing and growth.

3. Get a brief, chronological history of the divorce.

4. Assess the emotional response of family members to the divorce.

5. Identify problems the family may be experiencing.

6. Determine whether the divorce has hurt the parent's ability to raise the child effectively.

7. Assess family members' levels of cooperation and animosity.

8. Determine where the parent is in overcoming the trauma of divorce.

9. Assess the social, economic, and spiritual situations in the home.

10. Administer the Fisher Divorce Adjustment Scale to evaluate the level of the parent's adjustment. This test, written by Bruce Fisher, is available from the Family Relations Learning Center,

450 Ord Drive, Boulder, CO 80303. Cost of each test is $5, with an additional $2 charged for evaluation of each test. Consisting of 100 statements to be completed by the parent, the test is scored to rate the parent's adjustment concerning symptoms of grief, disentanglement from the love relationship, self-acceptance, and rebuilding social relationships.

SESSION 2: UNDERSTANDING CHILDREN'S REACTIONS TO DIVORCE

1. Explain that, as Archibald D. Hart indicates in *Children and Divorce,* a child can learn positive or negative reponses through a divorce. On the negative side, the child may learn to hate and distrust others, to be "sneaky," and to lie. On the positive side, he or she may learn to be loving and kind, forgiving, patient, and enduring.

2. Point out how children often use their emotions to get their needs met—to get special attention, to retaliate when they feel unfairly treated, and to protect themselves from further hurts.

3. Explain the reactions to divorce which children usually display at various age levels. Up to age six, for example, the child of divorce often displays fear, wants physical contact, has difficulty with peers, suffers lowered self-esteem, displays regressive behavior, retreats into fantasy, is confused or aggressive or guilty, and feels a loss of security.

From ages 7-12, the child whose parents have recently divorced or separated is likely to exhibit acute behavior changes at school. Grades may drop; the child may become more irritable, moody, aggressive, and possessive. Depression and aimlessness may also become problems, and the child may seem to "give up" easily.

A teenager, meanwhile, may respond to the failure of his parents' marriage by becoming angry and intolerant as well as depressed. The young person may withdraw, isolating himself from others, and may even try to run from his problems.

4. Explain that some of the child's responses may alarm the parent, though they are normal and common. These include physical illness, guilt feelings, emotional detachment, trying to manipulate the parents into a reconciliation, confusion, and expressing hatred toward the parents.

SESSION 3: IDENTIFYING YOUR CHILD'S NEEDS AND PROBLEMS

1. Discuss specific problems the parent finds at the moment in

his or her family. Possibilities include the following:
a) Poor communication
b) Conflict between parents involving children
c) Misbehavior by children
d) Negative emotional responses
e) Abuse or violence
f) Depression or fear on the part of children
g) Psychosomatic illness
2. Administer the Child Behavior Checklist to help you identify problem areas. This is a 118-item checklist for the parent that rates a child on nine problem behavior scales, three social competence scales, and two pathological dimensions. Written by Thomas M. Achenbach, Ph.D., the test is available from University Associates in Psychiatry, Department of Psychiatry, University of Vermont, One South Prospect St., Burlington, VT 05401. Cost of the Checklist is $25 for 100 tests; cost of the scoring profile is $25 for 100.

SESSION 4: YOUR CHILD AND SELF-ESTEEM

Cover the following principles, based on those set forth by Archibald Hart in *Children and Divorce*:
1. Point out that children of divorce often experience lowered self-esteem for one or more of the following reasons: The stigma of divorce, disruption of the family, lack of a climate of love in the home, or simply the child's depression.
2. To help the parent determine whether his or her child is suffering from low self-esteem, describe its common symptoms. They include timidity, bullying, anger, uncertainty about decisions, a "failure" attitude, and loss of hope for the future.
3. Suggest the following steps the parent can take to build self-esteem in the child:
a) Be kind but honest in responding to the child.
b) Teach that being imperfect is acceptable.
c) Don't set up standards the child can't meet.
d) Build the ego with unconditional love.
e) Learn to value the things your child does well.
f) Help your child learn to compensate for deficiencies.
g) Correct distorted peer feedback such as name-calling and rejection.
h) Teach that spiritual values, not physical attributes, reflect real beauty.

SESSION 5: YOUR CHILD AND NEGATIVE EMOTIONS

Begin by discussing the negative feelings the parent has observed in his or her child since the divorce or separation. Then point out the following facts and remedies regarding three of the most common negative emotions faced by children of divorce:

1. *Anxiety.* Explain that for children, divorce often produces feelings of abandonment, a loss of stability and security, separation, stigmatizing by peers, and fear of the future—any of which may produce anxiety. Symptoms of anxiety can include physical illness, temper tantrums, irrational fears, and withdrawal. Since the root cause of anxiety is insecurity, the parent needs to consistently remind the child that the parent's love and God's love are unconditional.

2. *Anger.* People become angry to protect themselves from hurt, to mask their true feelings, to express frustration, or to retaliate for real or imagined offenses against them. Parents of angry children should help their children express anger in constructive ways. This process begins as the parent spends time alone with the child, listening carefully and watching the child's body language for signs of hidden anger. The child should be helped to understand that anger is normal, but that it should be talked out rather than acted out. Finally, the parent needs to model acceptable ways to deal with anger, even during the frustrating season of divorce or separation.

3. *Depression.* Symptoms of depression include sadness, loss of interest in normal activities, discontent or frustration, and self-rejection. A child may display the latter by "putting himself down" verbally. The parent who wants to help overcome a child's depression should do the following:

a) Try to understand the child's point of view;
b) Accept depression as a normal reaction to divorce;
c) Give the child space and time to feel his or her loss;
d) Help the child accept the reality of the loss;
e) Pray with the child; and
f) Help the child move beyond the loss.

SESSION 6: DEVELOPING EFFECTIVE PARENTING SKILLS

1. Make the observation that to communicate effectively with a child, a parent needs to listen for *feelings,* not just words. Parents should make a habit of practicing healthy communication, which expresses acceptance, love and

concern—rather than blame, judgment, guilt, and defensiveness.
2. Administer the Single-Parenting Questionnaire. This is a testing instrument developed by Dr. Arnold Stolberg of the University of Virginia. It consists of 88 questions concerning the parent's interactions with the child, and rates problem solving, support systems, parental warmth, discipline and control, parental rules, and enthusiasm for parenting.

Counseling the Child: Six Sessions

Is it enough to counsel the parent, or does the child of divorce need such help, too? We believe it's important to give the child direct access to a counselor. As Archibald Hart writes in *Children and Divorce*, "Parents cannot always trust their own assessment; they have too strong a need to believe everything is OK."

A great deal can be accomplished through the six children's sessions that follow. We recommend that the child attend session one soon after his or her parent has attended the first parental session. After both initial meetings, the counselor will be better able to determine which of the remaining sessions, if any, are necessary for the child's recovery.

In deciding how much counseling a child needs, the counselor should consider the following factors:
1. The parent's adjustment to the divorce;
2. The availability of additional support for the child, such as children's workshops on divorce recovery (see chapter 6) and supportive role models and teachers in the church; and
3. The child's level of difficulty in overcoming his or her negative responses to the divorce.

SESSION 1: THE CHILD'S INITIAL INTERVIEW

In this session, the counselor seeks to assess the child's (1) developmental level, (2) understanding of and response to the divorce, (3) ability to cope, and (4) symptoms of divorce stress.
1. Discuss the facts of the divorce as the child sees them. If the child is reluctant to open up, it may be helpful to show him or her a prepared presentation on divorce, such as the slide/cassette program entitled, "The Sky Is Falling." This 20-minute, 65-slide presentation by Margaret Galante and Liane Leighton features brightly colored cartoons depicting the breakup of a "typical" couple and the resulting impact on their two children.

The set may be purchased for $30 from the Port Washington Union Free School District, 99 Compass Dr., Port Washington, NY 11050.

2. Find out what you can about how well the child is adjusting to the divorce. Having the child draw a picture of his or her family may help. Such a drawing often reveals the child's view of his or her relationship to other family members. Use the drawing to spark additional discussion.

SESSION 2: UNDERSTANDING HOW DIVORCE MAKES YOU FEEL

1. Discuss common responses children have to divorce at the child's particular age level (see parental counseling, session two).

2. Explain other reactions children of various ages often have to divorce (feelings of hatred toward parents, guilt, a desire to force a reconciliation of the parents, etc.). The following books provide additional information on this subject: *Helping Children of Divorce* by Neal C. Buchanan and Eugene Chamberlain, Broadman Press; and *Children and Divorce* by Archibald D. Hart, Word Books.

3. Talk over specific reactions the child is having to the divorce of his or her parents. Avoid the temptation to "correct" the child's feelings; listen carefully.

SESSION 3: LEARNING TO UNDERSTAND AND CONTROL ANGER

1. Ask the child to list five things about the divorce that make him or her angry. Then ask, "How do you usually respond when you feel this way? Can you think of a better response than the one you usually make?"

2. Provide several hand puppets from which the child may choose. Ask the child to make up scenes which show how he or she felt—or will want to feel—at the following times:

a) One year before the divorce;

b) At the time of divorce; and

c) One year after the divorce.

After the child uses the puppets, discuss the scenes. Help the child to envision more positive reactions to the anger he or she may feel over the divorce.

3. Discuss forgiveness with the child, showing how learning to forgive will dissolve anger and allow more positive emotions to emerge.

IMS

SES

1.   (see
par
2.   nd a
Bib   ok up
the   vhich
are
a)
b)
c)
d)
3.   ssion,
su   ivorce,
g   about
o   n these
a

INVENTORY CONTROL CARD
David C. Cook Publishing Co.
850 NORTH GROVE AVENUE ELGIN, ILLINOIS 60120
1-800/323-7543

LIST PRICE $ 6.95
D.C.C. ITEM NO. 67157
INTEREST LEVEL ADULT
BINDING TYPE PB
DATE RECEIVED
TITLE * CHILD OF DIVORCE—CRISIS SERIES
ISBN 0-89191-345-9
AUTHOR J & B DYCUS
MERCHANDISING CLASS PASTORS/CH LEADERS CHURCH GROWTH

1. Administer the _____ st to the child. This test, authored by E. V. Piers and P.B. _____, consists of 80 first-person statements to which the child responds yes or no; half the statements are worded to indicate a positive self-concept, and half negative. The test is available from Counselor Recordings and Tests, Nashville, TN.

2. Ask the child to complete the following: "Three things I like about myself are . . . ." "Three things I don't like about myself are . . . ." and "I wish I were more . . . ." Which of his or her answers does the child consider most important?

3. Discuss ways to build good self-esteem. Point out that being imperfect is all right, that we can accept failure and use it as a chance to grow, that we can learn to be good at some things, and that we can learn to make up for our weak points with God's help.

SESSION 6: LEARNING TO ADAPT TO CHANGES

1. Discuss ways in which the child feels his or her life has changed since the divorce. Encourage the child to write down your suggestions on how he or she could adapt positively to these changes.

2. Help the child prepare for future challenges with an exercise called "How Will I Act When I Feel. . . ?" Choose (or have the

child choose) emotions from the following list: mean, proud, happy, angry, lonely, sad, friendly, loving. You could even turn the choice of emotions into a game by writing the list on cards and asking the child to draw one, or by writing the list on a chart and having the child spin a pointer or toss a button to make the choice. Then roleplay situations in which the child responds to the emotions. Suggest alternate, positive responses as needed.

SESSION 4: ANXIETY AND DEPRESSION

1. Outline for the child some symptoms of depression (see parental counseling, session five).

2. For age seven and up: Give the child a piece of paper and a Bible (the King James Version works best in this case). Look up the following verses with the child, pointing out the things which are said to bring *happiness:*

a) Psalm 144:15 (having God as your Lord)
b) Proverbs 3:13 (wisdom and understanding)
c) Proverbs 16:20 (trusting the Lord)
d) John 13:17 (doing what God wants)

3. Discuss ways in which the child might overcome depression, such as realizing that feeling sad is a normal reaction to divorce, giving oneself time to feel the loss, and talking with God about one's feelings. Help the child set some personal goals in these areas.

SESSION 5: DEVELOPING GOOD SELF-ESTEEM

1. Administer the Piers Harris Self-Concept Scale Test to the child. This test, authored by E. V. Piers and P.B. Harris, consists of 80 first-person statements to which the child responds yes or no; half the statements are worded to indicate a positive self-concept, and half negative. The test is available from Counselor Recordings and Tests, Nashville, TN.

2. Ask the child to complete the following: "Three things I like about myself are . . . ." "Three things I don't like about myself are . . . ." and "I wish I were more . . . ." Which of his or her answers does the child consider most important?

3. Discuss ways to build good self-esteem. Point out that being imperfect is all right, that we can accept failure and use it as a chance to grow, that we can learn to be good at some things, and that we can learn to make up for our weak points with God's help.

SESSION 6: LEARNING TO ADAPT TO CHANGES

1. Discuss ways in which the child feels his or her life has changed since the divorce. Encourage the child to write down your suggestions on how he or she could adapt positively to these changes.

2. Help the child prepare for future challenges with an exercise called "How Will I Act When I Feel. . . ?" Choose (or have the child choose) emotions from the following list: mean, proud, happy, angry, lonely, sad, friendly, loving. You could even turn the choice of emotions into a game by writing the list on cards and asking the child to draw one, or by writing the list on a chart and having the child spin a pointer or toss a button to make the choice. Then roleplay situations in which the child responds to the emotions. Suggest alternate, positive responses as needed.

CHAPTER SIX

HOW YOUR CHURCH
CAN HELP

THE CHURCH—NOT JUST THE PASTOR OR A FEW LEADERS—
needs TO recognize its responsibility to help the victims of
divorce and separation rebuild their lives. After all, the
example of the New Testament Church is one of an involved,
caring, extended family:

And all the believers met together constantly and shared everything
with each other, selling their possessions and dividing with those in
need. They worshiped together regularly at the Temple each day, met
in small groups in homes for Communion, and shared their meals with
great joy and thankfulness, praising God. The whole city was favorable
to them, and each day God added to them all who were being saved
(Acts 2:44-47, TLB).

Those believers cared about each other, and about the whole
community. They understood that the Church was to stand in the
gap and help the one in need. Today's Church must do the same.

Hagar and Ishmael: A Model

Hagar and Ishmael (Gen. 21) were a single-parent family,
separated from Abraham, Ishmael's father. They suffered a
social stigma, as do many such families today. Yet God cared for
Hagar and Ishmael when they were ready to give up:

God heard the boy crying, and the angel of God called to Hagar from
heaven and said to her, "What is the matter, Hagar? Do not be afraid;
God has heard the boy crying as he lies there. Lift the boy up and take
him by the hand, for I will make him into a great nation."
Then God opened her eyes and she saw a well of water. So she went
and filled the skin with water and gave the boy a drink.
God was with the boy as he grew up. He lived in the desert and
became an archer (Gen. 21:17-20).

We can use the example of God's care for Hagar and Ishmael
as a model for the local church's ministry to the children of
divorce:

1. *We must recognize the need for ministry.* "God heard the boy crying" (v. 17).
2. *We must unconditionally accept children of divorce.* "Lift the boy up and take him by the hand" (v. 18).
3. *We must develop positive responses to a negative situation.* "I will make him into a great nation" (v. 18).
4. *We must respond to each person's unique needs.* "She . . . gave the boy a drink" (v. 19).
5. *We must encourage spiritual growth.* "God was with the boy as he grew up" (v. 20).

A Whole-Church Program for Recovery

In this chapter we will suggest how to go beyond individual counseling to involve groups—both volunteer helpers and victims of divorce—in the recovery process.

You will need to style your ministry to your unique setting, of course. One of your first tasks will be conducting a poll in your church and community to discover who is hurting and who can help.

Begin by asking the single-parent families in your church and/or community questions like these:

1. Do you feel there is a need in our church/community for workshops designed to help family members deal with the crisis of divorce?
2. Would you attend? Monthly, weekly, other?
3. Would you encourage your children to attend?
4. What topics would you like to discuss?
5. What are some of your personal concerns?
6. Do you have any suggestions or comments regarding such a program?

From those already involved in helping divorced families in your area, such as government agencies and charities, you will want to find out the following:

1. How many families of divorce are there in our area? What are their greatest needs?
2. What community resources, including agencies, services, classes, seminars, single-adult church activities, and written materials are already available to them?
3. How helpful are these existing resources, and how much do they cost?

Gaining Support

Even as the program is taking shape, based on the needs and resources revealed in the initial survey, the support of the church and community will be vital. Here are key people whose enthusiasm you'll need:

1. *The senior pastor.* In many instances, the degree of concern the senior pastor has for single-parent families will become that felt by much of the congregation. If you are not in this position yourself, you will need to gain the senior pastor's support to minister effectively to the divorced or separated family. He will be invaluable as you present your burden to the church.

2. *The church board and lay volunteers.* Your senior pastor can assist you in gaining the support of the board and volunteers in your congregation.

3. *The congregation.* Encourage your single parents to begin sharing their needs on a one-to-one basis with members of the congregation. Ask the senior pastor to make positive pulpit announcements about meeting the needs of single-parent families. Plan activities such as "Single Parents' Day," Christian big brother/big sister programs, and panels, forums, or seminars which will help your congregation become aware of single-parent needs.

4. *The community.* As your program develops, keep the following informed:
a) Community health centers
b) Social service agencies
c) Clergy from other churches
d) Medical professionals
e) Teachers
f) School counselors
g) Professional associations of those who work with children and youth
h) Courts
i) Other law professionals

Your program should be presented to these community groups as a resource for them, a complement to their own programs. This should help overcome any fear of competition they may feel. You will also need to develop your program's visibility in your community so that it can become a well-used, trustworthy addition to community efforts to reach the victims of divorce.

Recruiting Help

Your workers will, to a large extent, determine the success of a ministry to children of divorce. That's why recruiting and training must be undertaken with special care.

If you wish only to train present pastoral staff, Sunday school teachers, youth workers, and others to understand and help children of divorce within your current church program, your staff already will have been recruited. Your focus will be on training. But if you envision a special, additional program aimed at helping the single-parent family, you'll need to recruit workers as well.

Whom should you recruit? We believe the following are usually good prospects:

1. Those with experience in working with families and children in crisis;
2. Those who teach youth or children, either in school or in your church;
3. Those who have gone through divorce and have, in your estimation, made a good recovery from the experience—and have the spiritual maturity necessary for this ministry.
4. Others who are teachable and have expressed concern for children of divorce.

Training the Staff

We offer the following six sessions as one way to train your staff. Each session is designed to last about two hours; all six could be completed in six weeks, or during an intensive, two-day retreat or seminar. If you need more background in the subjects of the sessions, you may find the following publications useful: *Divorce Program Recovery Guide,* Jim and Barbara Dycus, 1199 Clay St., Winter Park, FL 32789 ($14.95); *When Your Relationship Ends,* Bruce Fisher, Family Relations Learning Center, 450 Ord Dr., Boulder, CO 80303 ($6); *Helping Children of Divorce,* Neal Buchanan and Eugene Chamberlain, Broadman Press, Nashville, TN; *Helping Youth and Families of Separation, Divorce, and Remarriage,* DHHS Publication #(OHDS) 80-32010, U.S. Department of Health and Human Services, Office of Human Development Services, Administration of Children, Youth, and Families, U.S. Government Printing Office, Washington, D.C. 20402.

Session 1: introduction

Begin the session with a get-acquainted time of informal conversation. After introducing those who will be leading the sessions, present an overview of the program planned for your church. Using the example of Hagar and Ishmael (see chapter 5 of this book), review the goals of your program.

Next, drawing on chapters 1 and 3, summarize the nature of the "season" of divorce and its implications for your church and community. Discuss the effect divorce and separation have had on your fellowship, especially among children. Explain the Biblical view of marriage and divorce.

Use the rest of the meeting to define what it will mean to be a leader in your church's program. Set goals for your leaders.

Session 2: understanding children's reactions to divorce

Using the case studies presented in chapter 2, explain how divorce tends to affect children. Summarize the following reactions children commonly have to divorce:

1. Grief
2. Insecurity
3. Fear
4. Guilt
5. Feelings of rejection
6. Anger
7. Confusion
8. Physical illness
9. Detachment
10. Trying to force a reconciliation

Divide the group into twos or threes. Assign each subgroup one of the aforementioned reactions and have them discuss how a child might display it, how a leader could respond, and how the child could be helped. Each subgroup should share its conclusions with the rest of the participants; the leader should help to correct misconceptions as needed.

Session 3: age-level symptoms of divorce stress

Explain that the following symptoms of divorce stress may be shown by children at the age levels indicated:

1. Preschool and kindergarten:
a) Desire for physical contact
b) Difficulty with peers

c) Low self-esteem
d) Loss of security
e) Fear
f) Regressive behavior
g) Fantasy
h) Confusion
i) Aggression
j) Guilt

2. Elementary:
a) Grief
b) Acute behavior shifts
c) Difficulties at school
d) Deep sense of loss of departed parent
e) Difficulty relating to peers
f) Anger
g) Tendency to give up
h) Aggression
i) Possessiveness
j) Depression

3. Adolescence:
a) Parent-child relationship changes
b) Worries about sex and marriage
c) Anger
d) Intolerance
e) Depression
f) Withdrawal and isolation

Divide the group into twos or threes. Ask each subgroup to roleplay a reaction covered in the presentation. The rest of the group, after watching each roleplay, should name the age level portrayed, the symptom exhibited, and responses leaders might make.

SESSION 4: DEALING WITH NEGATIVE EMOTIONS

Before the meeting, place throughout the room magazine pictures of children who exhibit various emotions. Ask trainees to walk around the room, look at the pictures, and select one. Each person should then tell the rest of the group about his or her picture, describing the emotion conveyed, the aspect of divorce that could make a child feel that way, and how a leader could help the child respond positively.

Using Mark 4:35-41, describe how Jesus calmed the storm when He and His disciples were in a boat. Jesus had said, "Let us go over to the other side" of the lake (v. 35), but when a storm arose the disciples panicked. They forgot that Jesus was going to take them to the other side. Make the point that the Lord wants divorce victims to get to the "other side" of recovery, and that He has the power to "calm the storm" of divorce.

Next, list steps your trainees can take to help divorce victims move from negative to positive emotions:
1. Providing unconditional acceptance;
2. Helping the family understand and pass through the grieving process of denial, anger, bargaining, acceptance, and growth;
3. Helping family members understand their emotions; and
4. Helping children accept the finality of the divorce.

Then ask group members to brainstorm for a few minutes, listing as many negative and positive expressions of emotion as they can. Conclude by going over the two lists together, showing where a positive expression can be substituted for a negative one.

Session 5: Understanding single-parent problems

Invite several single parents to the meeting. Allow time for informal conversation among parents and trainees.

Summarize as follows the challenges facing the single parent:
1. For the custodial parent:
a) Adjustment to singleness
b) Dual role as mother and father
c) Emotional and schedule overload
d) Financial changes
e) Changes in relationships
f) Dealing with the ex-spouse
g) Feelings of rejection
h) Wondering about God's will
i) Restoring stability and security for the child
j) Encouraging and understanding the child

2. For the noncustodial parent:
a) Adjustment to singleness
b) Finding housing

c) Financial changes
d) Establishing meaningful relationship with the child
e) Dealing with guilt
f) Wondering about God's will
g) Changes in relationships
h) Dealing with the ex-spouse

Next, have the single parents present a panel discussion concerning their needs. You'll need to prepare panel members in advance, instructing them to draw on their experiences for brief illustrations of the challenges they face. Conclude by having panel members field questions from the trainees.

SESSION 6: COMMUNICATING IN THE SINGLE-PARENT FAMILY

Begin by having each member of the group finish this sentence: "I want to minister to the single-parent family because. . . ."

Then outline and discuss the following ways to improve family communication:

1. Learn to listen for feelings, not just words.
2. Express acceptance, love, and concern rather than blame, judgment, and defensiveness.
3. Try creative ways to communicate with children, such as roleplaying, using puppets, expressing emotions through arts and crafts, using "icebreaker" activities to open communication lines, or reading and responding to a story.

Next, have the group brainstorm additional techniques that could speed recovery for victims of divorce. Take a few minutes to develop in detail one or two of the group's suggestions. Encourage your trainees to perfect and share other techniques as they get more involved in this ministry.

Close the session by praying as a group, committing yourselves to this ministry. Ask God to guide your group into the special approaches which will best meet the needs of the divorce victims in your church and community.

Adapting Your Current Church Program

Even without a specialized program for single-parent families, you can begin to make a difference by examining your existing church program from a divorce victim's point of view. Here are some changes you might make as a result:

1. Train teachers to include in their lessons illustrations and Bible stories about one-parent homes.

2. Visit single-parent homes represented in your church to develop a more caring, empathetic relationship with members of these families.

3. Be sure children of divorce are not excluded from church activities just because parental visitation schedules keep them from achieving perfect attendance, or because they lack transportation or funds, or because the "right" parent is unavailable (as in a father/son dinner).

4. Every teacher in your church should make a commitment to unconditionally love and accept each single-parent family in your church and community.

5. Exercise the belief that God can heal the hurts of divorce by encouraging your staff to focus on the wholeness of families in crisis—rather than treating them as second-class citizens or "emotional basket cases." Your emphasis in ministry should be to lead children of divorce and their parents to adapt positively to the changes they face.

Workshops for Children of Divorce

Group workshops for victims of divorce can be very helpful additions to your church program. They aid the formation of support networks as well as providing information to help victims toward recovery.

Much of the information in chapters 4 and 5, as well as the training sessions in this chapter, can be adapted for use in single-parent workshops. Since the focus of this book is the *children* of divorce, however, the remainder of this chapter offers meeting plans designed especially for them.

In the early days of our work with divorced families, we held workshops only for the adults; we baby-sat the children. But each week more and more children would attend, and more and more baby-sitters would quit! Finally we understood: God wanted us to *minister* to the children, not baby-sit them. This should be your goal as well, a goal embodied in the following objectives for the workshops:

1. Foster group feeling
2. Develop trust
3. Respect confidentiality
4. Develop open communication

5. Encourage spiritual stability

The six sessions which follow are designed for use with elementary school children. Suggested topics for teenagers are included at the end of the chapter; adapt them to create your own sessions.

SESSION 1: "I HURT!"

1. *Introduction (suggested remarks by the leader to the children):* Remember the very first time you climbed on your bike to try to ride it? Everyone said, "Oh, you can do it! There's nothing to it." You thought it looked so easy. You thought, "I'm going to get up on that seat and go sailing down the street—no sweat!"

What happened? Did the street jump up at you? Did something tip you over? Did you end up with a few hurts?

Divorce is like that. It hurts! Most of the time we don't understand what makes it hurt. Sometimes we pretend it doesn't hurt, and try to hide our sadness. But this won't help us find out what it is that hurts.

You couldn't ride your bike until you learned how to get on and off, to balance, to stop and start and go in a straight line. There's a lot you need to learn about divorce, too. We hope these next six lessons will help. And there's one more thing we want you to learn: God can heal your hurts!

2. *"This Is Me":* Ask each student to share information about himself or herself (name, school, parent with whom he lives, favorite things, etc.), either orally or as a writing exercise. Use this as a get-acquainted time.

3. *Memory Verse:* "Jesus said, 'Let the little children come to me, and do not hinder them' " (Mt. 19:14).

4. *Bible Story:* Jesus loves children (Matthew 19; Mark 10).

5. *Prayer Diary:* Have students make booklets with construction paper covers and plain white pages. Students should write in their booklets things they will pray about during the six sessions. These prayer concerns should relate to their divorce situations. For example, a student might pray that she or he will feel better about missing the parent with whom she or he no longer lives.

6. *Letters to God:* Have students write letters to God, telling Him three things that make them happy and three that make them sad. Students who express themselves more easily by drawing may do so.

Session 2: learning about divorce words

1. *Introduction:* Did a teacher at school ever ask you a question you couldn't answer just because you didn't understand the words she was using? Words can be confusing if you don't understand them. They can even be downright scary.

Divorce brings a lot of new and confusing words into our lives. Lots of times we may not understand what they mean. But we don't have to let them confuse or frighten us. We just need to talk about them and discover for ourselves what they mean.

That's what we're going to do today. We're going to look at the special words of divorce and find out about them. Then when you hear your parents or others discussing these words, you'll know what they mean.

2. *Memory Verse:* "He is a father to the fatherless. He gives families to the lonely" (Ps. 68:5, 6, TLB).

3. *Divorce terms:* Put the following divorce terms, along with scrambled versions of them, on a chalkboard, overhead transparency, or flip chart. Have students match each word with its scrambled version. As you discuss the answers, go over definitions for the terms to acquaint the children with their meanings:

Alimony (or Maintenance): An allowance given to help support one's divorced spouse

Child: Special person like you

Child Support: An allowance given to the parent in whose home you live

Court: People assigned by the government to decide justice

Court Hearing: The time for presenting a case to the court

Custody: The control and care of children

Decree: The legal paper which grants a divorce

Divorce: A legal breaking up of the marriage relationship

Father: The male parent

Family: People who live in one home

Home: The place where the family lives

Husband: A married man

Jesus: The One who heals our hurts

Judge: The officer who presides over the court

Lawyer (or Attorney): A person who helps us understand the laws and present a case in court

Mother: The female parent

Separation: Time during which a husband and wife live apart and perhaps (though not always) get a divorce

Spouse: A husband or wife

Visitation: The right of a divorced parent to visit the children who live with the other parent

Wife: A married woman

4. *Bible Story:* The Bible talks about one-parent homes (Ex. 22:22, 23; Deut. 24:19-21; James 1:27).

5. *Flash Cards:* Using flash cards you've prepared before the session, review the divorce terms mentioned earlier.

SESSION 3: FEELING SAD

1. *Introduction:* Probably all of us felt very sad when our parents divorced or separated. We may have felt so sad that we didn't want to play with our friends or even to eat. We may have forgotten our homework and sat around the house.

Maybe we even felt like crying all the time. Did you know it's all right to cry? Crying can help us feel better about things.

One of the important things to remember about being sad is that we won't *always* be sad. That big hurt we have because we miss our mom or dad so much will feel much better after a few months when all the changes are over, and we get used to the new things in our lives.

And do you know what? Someone very important will always be with us during these sad times. That Person is Jesus. He will never leave us—ever!

2. *Memory Verse:* "Nothing will ever be able to separate us from the love of God" (Rom. 8:39, TLB).

3. *Bible Story:* Jesus keeps the ship from sinking (Mk. 4:35-41). Explain that just as Jesus stayed with the disciples and exercised His power over the storm, He has promised to stay with us and bring us to "the other side" of troubles.

4. *Group Game:* Play a game which will help students understand what it means to cope with and compensate for losses. Have the students form a large circle; select one child to be the first player. He or she should stand in the center of the circle and do the following:

a) Say, "On my way home today, guess what I lost?"

b) Choose a body part and pretend it has been lost.

c) Act out a situation showing how difficult it would be to get along without that part. (Example: Hop on one foot to show loss of the other foot.)

After all students have participated, ask each to give an example of how he or she has learned to cope with living with just one parent at a time.

5. *A Letter to Yourself:* Have students write letters to themselves, describing how they feel about their parents' divorce, and how they want to feel about the divorce in four weeks. Give each student an envelope in which to seal his or her letter. Collect and hold the letters; they will be opened and discussed in the final session.

SESSION 4: WAS IT MY FAULT?

1. *Introduction:* Guilt doesn't feel very good. When we feel guilty, we feel it was our fault that something happened or didn't happen.

Sometimes we feel that way about our parents' divorce. We think maybe if we had been better they would still be together. We think maybe they wouldn't argue so much if we weren't around for them to argue about.

Or we remember those bad grades we brought home from school, or that fight we got into, and recall how disappointed our parents were. We think maybe if we had tried harder, there would have been no divorce. Sometimes we even wish we had never been born.

But did you know that kids can't solve their parents' grown-up problems? We need to learn that. We didn't make the divorce happen, and we can't put our parents back together. We have to learn to let our parents make their own choices about what they think is best for them.

2. *Memory Verse:* "We know that all that happens to us is working for our good if we love God" (Rom. 8:28, TLB).

3. *Cause and Effect:* List the following actions on the board or on handouts:

a) I yelled at Mom or Dad.
b) I didn't do what Mom or Dad told me to do.
c) I didn't try hard enough at school.
d) I caused a lot of work for Mom and Dad.
e) I got mad when Mom and Dad wouldn't let me do what I wanted.
f) I wished Mom and Dad would leave me alone.

Have students decide which of these actions they think caused their parents' divorce. Then discuss these feelings, helping the students understand that *none* of these actions was the cause.

4. *Bible Story:* Sometimes sad things happen that aren't our fault (the story of Job, as well as the story of the man born blind in John 9).

5. *Listening Circle:* Sit in a circle with the class. Explain that you are going to play a listening game which will help everyone begin to understand each other's feelings about divorce.

To begin, one student makes a simple statement: "My parents got a divorce." The second person repeats the sentence and adds one of his own: "I live with my mother." The third person repeats the first two sentences and adds another. Continue until someone repeats the sentences incorrectly.

6. *Finger Painting.* Talk briefly about guilt. Ask: Have you ever felt guilty about anything? Did you feel guilty because you really did something wrong? Has anyone ever said you did something that you really didn't do? How did that make you feel? Do you know that almost every person whose parents have divorced has felt guilty about it? Have you ever felt this way?

Explain that the group is going to do some finger painting. Each student is to paint a picture showing guilty feelings. Provide finger painting materials and allow students time to complete their work.

Most of the paintings will probably be abstract and meaningless to all but their creators, but the process of painting will require children to face their feelings about guilt.

When the paintings are done, encourage students to show them and to explain what they mean.

SESSION 5: 'I'M A BIG ZERO'

1. *Introduction:* Ever feel like a dummy? Not just because of something you did, but just about everything?

Divorce can make us feel pretty lousy. It can make a person feel like a big zero—a nobody. If we feel that way, we need to learn to like ourselves again.

The best way to feel good about ourselves is to find out how much Jesus loves us. His love is a very special gift to us, better than any other present we ever received.

2. *Memory Verse:* "See how very much our heavenly Father loves us, for he allows us to be called his children . . . and we really *are!*" (I Jn. 3:1, TLB).

3. *Do You Like Yourself?:* Pass out pencils and paper. Ask

students to complete the following sentences:
a) I like myself because . . . . (Give three reasons.)
b) I don't like myself because . . . . (Give three reasons)
c) I wish I were more . . . .

After allowing students time to complete the sentences, ask them to tell what they considered the most important thing they wrote about themselves.

4. *Bible Story:* A little boy is part of a big miracle (Jn. 6:1-14). Emphasize that the Lord values us and can use us even when we're young, and even when we don't seem to have much to offer Him.

5. *Appreciation Circle:* Have the class sit in a circle. Place a chair in the middle of the circle. Put a sign on the chair that reads, "Appreciation Seat."

Choose a student to sit in the appreciation seat. Go around the circle, having each student say to the person in the seat, "I appreciate you because . . . ." and adding something about the person. Do this with each student.

6. *Self-Images.* Before class, prepare a batch of flour-and-salt modeling dough (made of four cups flour, one cup salt, and a cup and a half of water). In class, give each student a piece of waxed paper on which to work; each student should make a "self-image" out of dough, showing how he or she sees himself. Afterward, allow time for each student to explain his or her image to the class.

SESSION 6: LEARNING TO BE ME

1. *Introduction:* Isn't it great to think about what we are going to be when we grow up? There are so many choices to choose from, so many occupations we could pick. Do you know who will help you make these and other important choices in your life? Listen to this: "I pray that Christ will be more and more at home in your hearts, living within you as you trust in him" (Eph. 3:17, TLB).

Sometimes we may wonder what's going to happen to us. We may even find it hard to think beyond the confusion we feel now because of divorce. But God wants to help us make right choices for the future. We can choose to be all God wants us to be— inside, where it counts!

2. *Memory Verse.* "When someone becomes a Christian he becomes a brand new person inside" (II Cor. 5:17, TLB).

89

3. *Bible Story.* Learning to make good choices (from the story of David in I Sam. 17, or the story of Joseph in Gen. 37-47). Show how honoring God led to success for one or both of these young men.

4. *Working Together.* Let students choose a project through which they will help the church in some way. Plan a specific time to carry out this activity, being sure to clear the project with appropriate church authorities.

5. *Career charades.* Have students choose careers they might enjoy, and then act them out without words for the rest of the group to guess.

6. *Letter reading.* Close by passing out the sealed letters students wrote during the third session. Encourage the letter writers to share their thoughts, with special emphasis on how their feelings about divorce have changed during the last few weeks. Discuss how God can continue to help your students reach their goals of recovery.

Workshops for Teenagers

Your church can also minister to teenagers whose parents are divorced or separated by designing sessions especially for them. Keep in mind that teens are likely to respond to a program that provides fellowship, is informal, and focuses on growth through building emotionally healthy life styles.

What topics should you cover? Find out which of the following questions are among those uppermost in your young people's minds, and base six or so sessions on them:

1. Why would people want to get a divorce?
2. How can I ever accept the changes in my family?
3. How can I stop feeling guilty and responsible for my parents' divorce?
4. What can I do about my anger and depression?
5. How can I be loyal to both my parents?
6. How can I let my parents know my needs?
7. What do I do about holidays and vacations?
8. Should I stop hoping my parents will get back together?
9. How can I form new relationships with family members and other kids?
10. How can I feel better about myself?
11. How should I set goals for my life?
12. Will I ever be able to have a happy marriage myself?

If your church serves a number of teens from broken homes, you may wish to form an ongoing support group for them. They should be encouraged to "stick with" the established youth group, however, rather than withdrawing. A support group, led by a youth worker with counseling experience, can be a valuable way station for teenage divorce victims on the road to recovery.

Chapter Seven

The Law and the Child of Divorce

THREE LEGAL ISSUES—CUSTODY, VISITATION, AND CHILD support—directly affect children of divorce. Anyone who wants to minister to these children needs to become familiar with these issues.

Divorce laws vary from state to state, and the way in which laws are applied can vary from court to court. This chapter provides a broad overview of the issues involved. We recommend contacting local legal professionals to determine law and practice in your area.

Custody

Some have predicted that by the end of the 1980s, half the children in the United States will live in one-parent homes before they reach age 18. Each of these children will be affected by the matter of custody.

Statute law does not define custody, but the following definition is in general use:

Custody of a minor embraces the sum of parental rights with respect to the rearing of the minor and connotes a keeping or guarding of the child. It includes in its meaning every element of provision for the physical, moral and mental well-being of the minor, including its immediate personal care and control *(Words and Phrases,* C. Edward Wall, Pierian Press).

Several types of custody may be awarded:

Sole custody. The court grants sole custody to one parent, with the other receiving visitation rights. The custodial parent remains in control of the rearing of the child, and determines the child's access to the noncustodial parent. Andre Bustanoby *(Being a Single Parent,* Zondervan) describes the battle for sole custody this way:

Even though a child's ongoing and frequent contact with both parents is important and even though either parent may be equally fit as primary care giver, the court must decide which parent will have sole custody. This conjures up the scene in Solomon's court where the two women laid claim to the same child (I Kings 3:16-28). The wisdom of Solomon is still needed today: the baby can't be cut in two. Yet, children are torn.

Joint custody. In theory, at least, parents with joint custody equally share decision-making authority regarding the child, even though the child resides with only one parent.
Divided or alternative custody. Under this arrangement, each parent has sole custody of the child for part of a year or in alternating years.
Split custody. This arrangement gives one parent custody of one or more children, and the other parent custody of the rest of the children.
Genuine shared custody. As outlined by Andrew Bustanoby, this arrangement uses a time-sharing formula whereby both parents are involved in all important decisions regarding the children, and maintain as much physical contact with them as circumstances and geography allow.

Mother or Father?

Hundreds of years ago, marriage and divorce were under the control of the church and ecclesiastical courts. A child was then viewed as property of the father, who was responsible for his or her physical care. When a marriage ended in divorce, it was practically predetermined that custody would be awarded to the father.

In 1839 the Talfourds Act was written in England, challenging the father's absolute authority. The court took over the right of determining custody for children under seven years of age, establishing a principle sometimes referred to as the "Tender Years Doctrine." Soon courts began to award custody of preschool children to mothers, not fathers. The trend continued until, by the early 1970s, several U.S. states required that the mother be preferred over the father no matter what the child's age, provided other factors (such as the "fitness" of each parent to care for a child) were equal.

Over the years, however, judges and lawyers voiced concern over the rights of children in these cases. This led to the "best interests" principle, which requires judges to award custody based on the best interests of the child.

The Judge's Discretion

Judges may exercise a high degree of freedom in making custody decisions. This power to choose makes these decisions especially difficult. As Robert Weiss observes:

The "best interests" principle requires that judges predict children's futures rather than evaluate evidence or decide facts or apply general legal principles to particular cases. In dealing with other legal issues, judges are required to go no further in their conclusions than evidence warrants; to decide custody they are asked to make long-term extrapolations from the present. Often they must weigh the relative merits of different kinds of life, and so must be willing to base decisions on values rather than evidence. Cases in which judges' values decide between mothers and fathers occur frequently and receive no public attention (*Divorce and Separation: Context, Causes, and Consequences*, George Levinger and Oliver C. Moles, editors, Basic Books, Inc.).

How do judges decide? In a 1982 article ("Child Custody Decisions: Content Analysis of a Judicial Survey" by Shirley A. Settle and Carol Lowery, *Journal of Divorce,* fall/winter issue), 57 judges and 23 commissioners in Kentucky named 20 factors which influence a judge's decision in child custody cases. They are listed in order of the weight respondents gave them in the survey:

1. Mental stability of each parent
2. Each parent's sense of responsibility to the child
3. Biological relationship to the child (when one parent is a stepparent)
4. Each parent's moral character
5. Each parent's ability to provide stable involvement in a community
6. Each parent's affection for the child
7. Keeping the child with brothers/sisters
8. Each parent's ability to provide access to schools
9. Keeping a young child with the mother
10. Physical health of each parent
11. The wishes of the parents
12. Professional advice
13. Biological relationship to the child (when one parent is adoptive)
14. Each parent's financial sufficiency
15. The child's wishes

16. Length of time each parent has had custody
17. Each parent's ability to provide contact with the child's other relatives
18. Each parent's ability to provide access to other children of about the same age
19. Each parent's ability or intention to provide a two-parent home
20. Placing a child with the parent of the same sex

The survey takers also noted, "Many of the respondents indicated that after taking everything into consideration, the final decision was made on their gut reaction to the individual case."

Mediation

Sometimes a mediator, rather than a trial judge, resolves custody questions. Mediation has been defined as "the process by which a couple, separated or preparing to separate, meet together with a trained third party, the mediator, to discuss and decide the issues involved in a separation agreement—child and spousal support, division of marital assets and debts and custody and visitation" ("Family Mediation: A Descriptive Case Study" by Jennifer Mannocherin, *Journal of Divorce,* spring/summer 1985 issue).

At least 24 states now have Conciliation Courts to mediate in custody cases. We believe these services have opened the door for Christian leaders and professionals to affect the decision-making process before the actual custody judgment is made. Here the church can help prevent some of the problems which hurt children of divorce. Meyer Elkin writes, "Since their inception, Conciliation Courts have used . . . back-up community services when referrals were needed and accepted by clients. The court's service and the community's services have not duplicated each other nor has there been a feeling of competition. The relationship has always been a complementary one rather than competitive" ("The Missing Links of Divorce Law: A Redefinition of Process and Practice," *Journal of Divorce,* fall/winter 1982 issue).

Joint Custody: A Solution?

Joint custody has been heralded by many professionals as the answer to the custody dilemma. But other experts express concern that joint custody will not work in many cases.

Proponents of joint custody cite its positive aspects, which may alleviate some of the trauma of divorce for a child. According to Andre Bustanoby (*Being a Single Parent*), joint custody is said to reduce the devastating effects of separation from a parent, feelings of personal loss, abandonment, rejection, loneliness, sex-role difficulties, antisocial acting out, delinquency, and depression. It increases two-parent involvement in the lives of the children, eliminates adversarial litigation, reduces parental conflict, and makes substitute parental care possible.

On the negative side, Bustanoby writes, other professionals list the limitations of joint custody. For example, joint *legal* custody without joint *physical* custody makes a parent legally responsible for a child, but provides limited opportunities to guide the child. Furthermore, it is disruptive for a child to have two homes instead of one, and a child's loyalties may be tested by the parents' continuing dislike of each other. Finally, opponents say, divorced parents will not cooperate. If the parents can get along so well with a joint-custody arrangement, why did they divorce? Clearly, joint custody is no cure-all for the disruption children experience when their parents divorce.

Several factors should be considered when deciding whether joint custody is best in a specific divorce, according to one study ("Joint Custody Reconsidered: Systematic Criteria for Mediation" by Sandra S. Volgy and Craig A. Everett, *Journal of Divorce,* spring/summer 1985 issue):

1. The parents' values and attitudes.
2. Their ability to tolerate differences in parenting.
3. The personal and emotional stability of each parent.
4. Both parents' ability to accept responsibility for their own actions.
5. The degree of trust the parents report in each other's parenting ability.
6. How motivated both parents are to provide continual access to the children of the other parent regardless of whether it is convenient or comfortable for them to do so.
7. Each parent's current and future capacity for required parenting skills and for comfortably sharing the children.
8. Intergenerational family ties.
9. The ability of both parents to withdraw their emotional attachment from the failed marital relationship.

10. Each parent's ability to integrate comfortably into new relationships and friendships.
11. The similarity of boundaries (values, expectations, etc.) which exists between both homes.

The Child's Best Interests

The Uniform Marriage and Divorce Act of 1974 gives judges the power to determine the best interests of the child in deciding custody. It includes provision for judges to interview children in their chambers, appoint guardians to represent children, and call on mental health professionals for assistance. But according to a 1983 study, these options are rarely exercised by judges.

Professionals disagree over whether the preferences of children should be established before the custody decision is made. At least two states have required judges to honor a statement of preference by an older child, and many other states indicate that a child's preference is a factor to be considered by judges. But some question how children, who are not recognized as mature in other areas, can be assumed to know which parent is "best" for them.

In any case, we who minister to children of divorce should affirm these children's rights, and provide the best possible framework for them to recover from their hurts. The following "Children's Bill of Rights," adapted from a decision of the Wisconsin Supreme Court, is worth keeping in mind as we seek to help these victims of divorce and separation.

Each child has the right to . . .

1. be treated as an interested and affected person and not as a pawn, possession, or chattel of either or both parents.
2. grow to maturity in that home environment that will best guarantee an opportunity for the child to grow to mature and responsible citizenship.
3. receive day-by-day love, care, discipline and protection of the parent having custody of the child.
4. know the noncustodial parent and have the benefit of such parent's love and guidance through adequate visitation.
5. have a positive and constructive relationship with both parents, with neither parent permitted to degrade or downgrade the other in the mind of the child.
6. have moral and ethical values developed by precept and practice and to have limits set for behavior so that the child early

in life may develop self-discipline and self-control.

7. receive the most adequate level of economic support that can be provided by the best efforts of both parents.

8. have the same opportunities for education that the child would have had if the family unit had not been broken.

9. receive periodic review of custodial arrangements and child support orders as the circumstances of the parents and the benefit of the child may require.

10. the recognition that children involved in a divorce are always disadvantaged parties, and that the law must take affirmative steps to protect their welfare.

Visitation

The second legal issue affecting children of divorce is visitation. It is also the second "battleground" for divorcing couples. As Robert Weiss writes:

With increasing experience of the consequences of custody decisions, it has been recognized that court decisions do not so much end the disputes of divorcing parents as they change their terms. Where before custody adjudication parents might battle over who might have the children, after custody adjudication they are likely to battle over the times and conditions of visitation. This recognition of the persistence of dispute has brought with it realization that there is inconsistency in the award of full custodial responsibility to one parent and visitation rights to the other (*Divorce and Separation: Context, Causes, and Consequences,* edited by George Levinger and Oliver C. Moles, Basic Books, Inc.).

Terms of visitation vary widely. The goal of visitation, however, should always be to maintain an ongoing, nurturing relationship between the child and both parents. Christian leaders must help parents who are at odds over visitation or custody. Children need both parents, and the church can help parents develop positive alternatives to conflict.

Special Concerns for Christians

Many Christian parents struggle with the ramifications of visitation as well as custody. Often only one parent is a Christian, and the other parent is not living a life of which the Christian parent approves. In these cases, the Christian parent may fear that the children will suffer spiritually by association with the non-Christian parent.

There are no easy answers to this problem, but the church must stand ready to assist parents in resolving their fears. Many times this may require a compromise between our preferences and the child's need for both parents. At other times the Christian parent will simply have to commit these fears to God and allow Him to resolve the problem.

In isolated cases, serious violation of a child's religious upbringing can result in loss of custody or visitation rights. But this is the exception, not the rule.

Making Visitation Work

Those who work with single parents can help prevent and solve visitation conflicts by passing along the following advice abridged from Andre Bustanoby's *Being a Single Parent:*

1. Don't argue with what the other parent may have told your child.
2. Don't try to cut down the child's positive image of the other parent.
3. Don't try to persuade the child that you are always right and the other parent is wrong.
4. Don't react defensively when the child reports that the other parent is telling unkind stories about you.
5. Don't attempt to get the child to offend the religious, moral, or social values of your ex-spouse.
6. Don't turn times of picking up and dropping off into opportunities to argue or attack.
7. Don't change plans capriciously.
8. Don't expect or allow your child to "spy" on the other parent.
9. Do listen to what your child is saying and take a friendly interest in him.
10. Do answer questions in a way that minimizes conflict.
11. Do be aware of any problems your child may have and what you can do about them.
12. Do be available on a reliable basis.
13. Do show that you have consistent standards of behavior.
14. Do make a visit enjoyable rather than looking at it an an opportunity to impress your child.
15. Do have your child ready for the visit.
16. Do understand that emergencies arise that require a change in plans.

17. Do be as friendly and courteous to your ex-spouse as you are with other adults.
18. Do remember that your ex-spouse loves the children, too.

Child Support

Child support is the single most frustrating concern many single parents face. The custodial parent who has been awarded child support by the court often struggles with the ex-spouse's failure to make the payments—or with the inadequacy of the payments to meet the family's financial needs. The noncustodial parent who must make the payments struggles with hostility and bitterness because he must support children he sees only occasionally. Many times the payments are a financial burden for the noncustodial parent; he may be supporting two households and paying divorce settlement obligations as well.

Statistics regarding child support are dismal. Only half of court-mandated support is ever paid. When it is, it amounts to an average of $1,800 a year. All this adds up to financial crisis for the single-parent family.

The church can help divorced parents cope with financial burdens. While in many cases we cannot greatly improve the financial status of these families, we can help them face the realities of a smaller-than-desired budget. We can point the family to agencies which stand ready to help, as well as to laws and programs that will assist the parent in living up to divorce settlement stipulations. Here are some of those laws and programs, together with others affecting custody judgments:

1. *Uniform Reciprocal Enforcement Support Act.* Administered by local district attorneys, this provides a method of enforcing support when the paying parent is in another state.

2. *Uniform Enforcement of Foreign Judgments Act.* This provides a way to enforce a judgment for visitation or support if the custodial or supporting parent is in another state.

3. *Uniform Child Custody Jurisdiction Act.* Most states have enacted some form of this law, which is designed to resolve interstate custody jurisdiction.

4. *Job Training Partnership Act.* This law provides training for displaced homemakers under Title II: Training Services for the Disadvantaged.

5. *Unemployment Compensation Intercept for Child Support.* All states are now required to have a program of this type in

effect for obtaining past-due support by withholding unemployment compensation under the Omnibus Reconciliation Act of 1981.

6. *Federal Parental Kidnapping Prevention Act.* This 1981 act requires that all state courts follow the jurisdictional standards of the Uniform Child Custody Jurisdiction Act. It directs the Justice Department to assist in the apprehension of parents if they violated state felony laws in removing a child to another state.

7. *Court-connected Marriage and Family Counseling Services (Conciliation Courts).* These mediation services, designed to complement divorce courts, are found in about 24 states.

8. *Federal Parent Locator Service.* Operated by the Health and Human Services Office of Child Support Enforcement, this service helps locate absconding parents through access to the address files of the Social Security Administration, Internal Revenue Service, Department of Defense, and other federal agencies.

9. *I.R.S. Diverted Funds for Back Payment of Child Support.* The nonpaying parent stands in contempt of court. He or she is subject to being hailed into court or having a federal tax refund diverted by the Internal Revenue Service for child support.

Beyond Laws

Laws and programs cannot do it all, of course. One of the greatest needs today is for law professionals and Christian leaders to communicate more effectively for the common good of the victims of divorce. Christian leaders need to develop working relationships with attorneys and judges in their communities. They need to understand each other's roles and the advantages, disadvantages, and limitations they have in serving the single-parent family. Many could benefit greatly from such a relationship—not least among them the most innocent victims of divorce, the children.

We Christians need to remember the fable about a cave that talked to the sun. Living underground, as caves usually do, the cave had spent its lifetime in darkness. One day it heard the sun say, "Come up into the light!"

The cave retorted, "What? There is nothing but darkness. Come and see."

The sun accepted the invitation. Entering the cave, it said,

"Show me your darkness." But there was none; the sun had dispelled it.

The presence of the Son can dispel the darkness surrounding the children of divorce. With His help, we can bring His healing light into their lives.

Achenback, Thomas M., 1966. *Child Behavior Checklist* (a psychological testing instrument). Burlington, Vt.: University Associates in Psychiatry, Department of Psychiatry, University of Vermont.

Bustanoby, Andre, 1985. *Being a Single Parent.* Grand Rapids, Mich.: Zondervan Publications.

Carter, Velma Thorne, and Leavenworth, Lynn J., 1985. *Caught in the Middle: Children of Divorce.* Valley Forge, Pa.: Judson Press.

"Children's Bill of Rights." Adapted from a decision of the Wisconsin Supreme Court.

Collins, Gary, 1980. *Christian Counseling: A Comprehensive Guide.* Waco, Tex.: Word Books.

Despert, J. Louise, 1953. *Children of Divorce.* New York: Doubleday and Co.

Dycus, Barbara, 1986. *God Can Heal My Owies* (curriculum for ages 2-6) and *God Can Heal My Hurts* (for ages 7-12). Winter Park, Fla.: Calvary Assembly.

Dycus, Jim and Barbara, 1981. *Divorce Program Recovery Guide.* Winter Park, Fla.: Self-published.

Elkin, Meyer. "The Missing Links in Divorce Law: A Redefinition of Process and Practice." *Journal of Divorce,* Vol. 6, Nos. 1/2 (fall/winter 1982).

Fisher, Bruce, 1982. *Fisher Divorce Adjustment Scale* (a psychological testing instrument). Boulder, Colo.: Family Relations Learning Center.

Fugate, J. Richard, 1980. *What the Bible Says About Child Training.* Tempe, Ariz.: Aletheia Publications.

Galante, Margaret, and Leighton, Liane. *The Sky Is Falling* (20-minute slide and cassette presentation). Port Washington, N.Y.: Port Washington Free School District.

Gendler, Mary L. "The Wild World of Divorce: Puppet Plays with Children of Divorce and Separation" (unpublished).

Hart, Archibald, 1982. *Children and Divorce*. Waco, Tex.: Word Books.

Henry, Matthew, 1706. *A Commentary on the Whole Bible*. Old Tappan, N.J.: Fleming H. Revell Co.

Levinger, George, and Moles, Oliver C., eds., 1979. *Divorce and Separation: Context, Causes, and Consequences*. New York: Basic Books.

Mannocherin, Jennifer. "Family Mediation: A Descriptive Case Study." *Journal of Divorce*, Vol. 8, Nos. 3/4 (spring/summer 1985).

Piers, E. V., and Harris, P. B., 1969. *Piers-Harris Self-Concept Scale* (a psychological testing instrument) Nashville, Tenn.: Counselor Recordings and Tests.

William Robertson, 1835. *The History of the Discovery and the Settlement of America*. Harper Press. Quoted by Hill, Verna M., 1960, in *The Christian History of the Constitution of the United States of America: Christian Self-Government*. San Francisco: Foundation for American Christian Education.

Settle, Shirley A., and Lowery, Carol R. "Child Custody Decisions: Content Analysis of a Judicial Survey." *Journal of Divorce*, Vol. 6, Nos. 1/2 (fall/winter 1982).

Stolberg, Arnold, 1981. *Single Parenting Questionnaire* (a psychological testing instrument). Richmond, Va.: Department of Psychology, University of Virginia.

Stolberg, Arnold L., and Anker, James M. "Cognitive and Behavioral Changes in Children Resulting from Parental Divorce and Consequent Environmental Changes." *Journal of Divorce*, Vol. 7, No. 2 (winter 1983).

Volgy, Sandra S., and Everett, Craig A. "Joint Custody Reconsidered: Systemic Criteria for Mediation." *Journal of Divorce*, Vol. 8, Nos. 3/4 (spring/summer 1985).

Wall, C. Edward, 1969. *Words and Phrases*. Ann Arbor, Mich.: Pieran Press.

Wallerstein, Judith S., and Kelly, Joan Berlin, 1982. *Surviving the Breakup: How Children and Parents Cope with Divorce*. New York: Basic Books, Inc.

Weinglass, Janet, Kressel, Kenneth, and Deutsch, Morton. "The Role of Clergy in Divorce: An Exploratory Survey." *Journal of Divorce*, Vol. 2, No. 1 (fall 1978).

Weiss, Robert, 1977. *Marital Separation: Managing After a Marriage Ends*. New York: Basic Books, Inc.

Additional Resources

Brandt, Patricia, with Jackson, Dave, 1985. *Just Me and the Kids* (a 13-week course in the Family Ministries Series, designed for single parents). Elgin, Ill.: David C. Cook Publishing Co.

The Family: Loving It Through Pain and Change (Vol. 8 in the *Pacesetter* series for senior high youth workers), 1987. Elgin, Ill.: David C. Cook Publishing Co.

Additional Resources

[faded, illegible text]